# Seances &
# Spiritualists

CHRISTINE ANDREAE

# Seances & Spiritualists

J. B. Lippincott Company
Philadelphia and New York

# ACKNOWLEDGMENTS

Pictures appearing on pages 13, 50, 123, courtesy of the New York Public Library Picture Collection; page 15, courtesy of The Bettmann Archive; pages 23, 27, 30, 31, 32, 40, 66, 97, and 98, courtesy of the Library of Congress; page 73, courtesy of World Wide Photos; page 92, rendered by Tom Huffman; page 105, courtesy of Howard Mitchell of Mankind Research Unlimited, Inc.; pages 108, 115, courtesy of the Association for Research and Enlightenment; page 149, courtesy of Paul Sauvin of Mankind Research Unlimited, Inc.

*133.9*

*AND*

U.S. Library of Congress Cataloging in Publication Data

Andreae, Christine.
    Seances & spiritualists.

    (The Weird and horrible library)
    SUMMARY: Describes the various aspects of spiritualism and some of its more famous practitioners.
    Bibliography: p.
    1. Spiritualism—Juvenile literature. [1. Spiritualism]   I. Title.
BF1261.2.A5          133.9          74–8044
ISBN–0–397–31555–4     ISBN–0–397–31583–X (pbk.)

# Contents

22669

# Introduction

SINCE ANCIENT TIMES, certain rare individuals have possessed powers which seemed to defy the established laws of nature. Whether they were witches or high priests, saints or shamans, their prophetic visions, their magic, and their miracles commanded fear and admiration. They were a breed apart whose special gifts had flowered only after intense initiations or years of meditation and study.

In the mid-nineteenth century, however, when Queen Victoria was on the throne of England and Americans were moving West in search of gold, thousands of ordinary people began showing signs of extraordinary talent. The air seemed charged with psychic energy. Shopkeepers and housewives, maiden aunts and schoolboys suddenly discovered they could tip tables without touching them, read minds, predict the future.

Because these people claimed that all their powers came directly from the spirits of the dead, they were called spirit mediums. They displayed their gifts at seances—a French word meaning "sittings." Seances were customarily held in a dark parlor where the medium and his or her guests sat around a table holding hands while the spirits manifested themselves. Mediums and their followers soon became known as "spiritualists."

Not all mediums, of course, had genuine psychic ability. There were many fakes, some ingenious, others clumsy, who went into the spirit business for money and prestige. Although the scientifically-minded exposed numerous frauds, the public romance with spiritualism persisted. For about fifty years, mediums enjoyed a Golden Age. Then, around the turn of the century, the cult began to die out.

Today, the upsurge of interest in the occult has given spiritualism a boost. Thanks to new scientific discoveries and inventions, however, it has undergone a change. Modern mediums are generally more interested in developing their extrasensory perception than in tipping tables in the dark. Many hold "meditation circles" instead of "seances" and communicate with "energy essences" instead of "spirits." Messages from family ghosts are considered somewhat déclassé; reincarnation and astral projection are in vogue.

Although the following pages deal with mediums and spiritualism in a roughly historical order, this book is by no means a history. It is simply an introduction to some of the more intriguing people and phenomena connected with spiritualism.

# Seances &
# Spiritualists

# 1

## Hypnosis and the Higher Phenomena: A Prelude to Spiritualism

SPIRITUALISM FLOWERED in the nineteenth century, but its roots go back to the eighteenth century when an Austrian doctor named Anton Mesmer accidently discovered hypnosis. (Hence the word "mesmerize.") Mesmer was a solid, middle-class citizen of no particular brilliance who enjoyed a conventional medical practice in Vienna. He had a taste for music, and his wife's money allowed him the luxury of patronizing young musicians including the twelve-year-old Mozart, whose first opera was performed in the doctor's garden. In 1774, when Mesmer heard reports that a Jesuit professor at the University of Vienna, one Father Maximilian Hehl, had worked astonishing cures using magnets, he was intrigued enough to try it out on one of his own patients.

He selected a young lady, Fraulein Oesterlin, who was subject to attacks of "hysteria." Certainly she presented a challenging bundle of symptoms: fainting, vomiting, depression, temporary blindness and paralysis, hallucinations, and convulsions. Mesmer hung a heart-shaped magnet around her neck, tied two more magnets to her feet, and watched as she suddenly fell into a convulsive fit. He was astonished to find that she was cured when she came to.

11

Magnetism was to Mesmer's day what atomic energy is to ours: it was a new phenomenon, and no one knew exactly what it could do. Mesmer theorized that magnets could convey an invisible healing fluid from the atmosphere to his patients. But after further experiments, he found he could also work cures with his hands. This led Mesmer to think he had discovered a special brand of magnetism, a human field of force, which he dubbed "animal magnetism."

In the following years, animal magnetism became the rage of Europe. The respectable Viennese doctor transformed himself into a kindly wizard who paraded before his fans in a lavender robe embroidered with gold flowers. To accommodate his booming practice, he invented a contraption called the baquet, which allowed him to treat thirty people at once.

This machine was a huge circular wooden tub filled with bottles of "magnetic fluid" and covered with a lid. Poking up through the lid were little iron rods which were supposed to give off a magnetic charge. Patients would enter Mesmer's luxuriously furnished apartment and take seats around the rim of the baquet, where they held onto the iron rods. The room was dimly lit and a small orchestra played soothing background music. At the strategic moment Mesmer would appear carrying an elaborate wrought iron staff. Sometimes, a simple wave of his wand was enough to work his cure. Other times, he would stroke his patients one after the other. An eyewitness described his technique: "Erecting his fingers in a pyramid, Mesmer passed his hand down over the patient's body, beginning with the head and going down over the shoulder to the feet. He then stroked the head again and also the stomach and the back. He repeated this process until, in his opinion, the magnetized person was saturated with healing fluid and was transported with pain or pleasure."

*Mesmer's baquet*

These "transports" of pain or pleasure usually took the form of orgiastic convulsions. Patients would writhe in agony or ecstasy, scream, cry, or even vomit. Then they would collapse in exhaustion. Although Mesmer admitted that his method didn't work for everyone, the majority of his patients came out of the ordeal relieved of their symptoms.

To Mesmer, the convulsions were the key to his cure. He believed that no one could be healed without experiencing the cathartic crisis. But today it is generally thought that the preliminary hypnotic stroking coupled with Mesmer's power of suggestion probably caused the sensational cures.

The general public found Mesmer's treatment an exciting novelty. But the medical profession, alarmed by the popular doctor's methods and disgusted by his theatrical flare, condemned animal magnetism as quackery. It was, they declared, a menace to public health and morals. It wasn't until one of Mesmer's pupils, a French nobleman called the Marquis de Puysegur, demonstrated that animal magnetism could cure without causing the "hellish convulsions" that men of science began to show interest in it.

Puysegur had paid Mesmer a fee of 100 gold louis to learn his secret. After his apprenticeship, the Marquis declared he was still a bit in the dark about how animal magnetism worked, but he was adept enough at it to cure his gamekeeper's wife of a toothache. He was also pleasantly surprised to find his treatment had no violent effects.

Then, on May 4, 1784, he proceeded to magnetize a young peasant boy named Victor who was suffering from a mild case of pleurisy. To Puysegur's astonishment, Victor responded by falling into a deep sleep. The boy began to babble about his worries, whereupon Puysegur reassured him and urged him to think of something more pleasant. Victor obediently began to jiggle, as if he were dancing at a village carnival. After a while he began to sweat. Puysegur calmed him down, left the room, and returned the next morning to find Victor's health much improved. Puysegur had stumbled across hypnosis as we know it today.

By 1825, French magnetists had described all the major phenomena of hypnosis: its power to mask pain, to make the body

*A hypnotized woman suspended by two chairs*

as rigid as steel, to induce hallucinations, and to persuade the subject to carry out the hypnotist's suggestions. As modern scientists readily admit, we know little more about hypnosis today than did the early experimenters. For although doctors have used hypnosis in psychiatry and dentistry, in obstetrics and weight-watching, they have been unable to discover why it works or what it is. "Hypnosis is no easier to define than love," snapped one scientist at a symposium on hypnotism. However, researchers most often describe it as a state of awareness somewhere between waking and sleeping. Although it is believed that everyone is capable of reaching this state in some degree, the ability to experience the deepest levels of hypnosis differs from person to person, just as the ability to play football or learn languages differs among a classroom of students.

In general, however, studies show that children, particularly between the ages of eight and twelve, tend to reach greater depths than adults over eighteen. Recent tests show men and women are equally susceptible, although for a long time it was thought that women were more easily entranced than men—perhaps because women were supposed to have weaker wills. Ernest R. Hilgard, a prominent American psychologist who has done some research on hypnosis, lists certain personality traits that susceptible people seem to have in common: they are adventurous spirits who reach out for new horizons of experience; they are less interested in competition than in the life of the mind; and they often act on impulse rather than reason.

In the hypnotic state, subjects are extremely open to suggestions given by the hypnotist. "Your voice came in my ear and filled my head" and "My thoughts were an echo of what you were saying" are two typical descriptions. Many subjects feel a compulsion to do whatever the hypnotist tells them. Subjects are also generally more passive than they are when in an ordinary waking state. Many feel no desire to move or speak. Fantasies and past memories tend to pop into the mind with vividness and ease, while everyday reality often becomes distorted. "My head sank into my body like a black sponge," one subject commented. Another said, "I felt as though I were 'inside' myself; none of my body was touching anything." Still another declared: "When I was deepest, I was down in the bottom of a dark hole. I turned over and over on the way down. Now and then I would float up toward the top of the hole."

This state of mind in which ordinary reality seems to be suspended was fertile ground for the growth of spiritualism. Early magnetists found that certain subjects, when placed in a trance, experienced ecstatic visions of heaven during which they claimed to be able to communicate with spirits of deceased relatives and friends. In the early 1800s, for example, Alphonse Cahagnet, a French cabinet maker, worked with a subject named Bruno, who on one occasion found himself "in a place without any horizon, illuminated by a superb light." On a throne before him, Bruno recognized God, gray bearded and crimson robed, while all around walked shining spirits. "Oh!" rhapsodized Bruno. "How ugly are the men of the earth in comparison with those beautiful faces, those fair skins. . . ."

Interest in the spiritual side of hypnosis was reinforced by the discovery of what magnetists called the "higher phenomena" of hypnosis. Men like Puysegur observed that hypnosis produced not only medical cures, but startling examples of telepathy (mind reading) and clairvoyance (eyeless vision). After many experiments with Victor, the Marquis wrote: "I have no need to speak to him. I merely think and he both understands and replies." Another of his subjects, a girl called Madeleine, frequently demonstrated her ability to "see" things when her eyes were tightly bandaged.

Although many early observers believed that hypnosis actually caused clairvoyance and telepathy, in the 1880s the famous and daring American psychologist William James concluded from his work with the spirit medium Mrs. Piper that hypnotic trance simply made psychic phenomena more likely to occur than the ordinary waking state. Whatever the necessary condition was, Mrs. Piper, like most mediums, had the knack of getting herself into it without any help from a hypnotist. In fact, she produced better results on her own than she did when James placed her in a hypnotic trance.

Today, hypnosis rarely, if ever, produces the higher phenomena. Although reports of telepathic hypnosis have come out of Russia in the last decade, most Western scientists, who are skeptical about the existence of psychic phenomena to begin with, generally dismiss accounts of hypnotic telepathy and clairvoyance as the effects of faulty observation and credulity. Nonetheless, nineteenth-century experimenters give some convincing evidence for the psychic side effects of hypnosis.

James R. Cook of Boston, a blind physician, was a cautious investigator who, unlike most mesmerists in his day, had subjected himself to hypnosis so he could better understand it. He believed hypnotism was useful in the treatment of certain disorders (alcoholism, insanity, overwork, headaches, and nausea, for example), but warned against thinking of it as a cure-all. He conducted many probing experiments, including the following telepathy test:

"I told the subject to remain perfectly still for five minutes and to relate to me at the end of this time any sensation he might experience. I passed into another room and closed the door and locked it; went into a closet in the room and closed the door after me; took down from the shelf, first a linen sheet, then a pasteboard box, then a toy engine, owned by a child in the house. I went back to my subject and asked him what experience he had had.

"He said, 'I seemed to go into another room and from thence into a dark closet. I wanted something off the shelf, but did not know what. I took down from the shelf a piece of smooth cloth, a long pasteboard box and a toy engine.' These were all sensations he had experienced."

The blind doctor asked his subject if he had seen the articles with his eyes.

"He answered that the closet was dark, and that he only felt them with his hand. I asked him how he knew that the engine was a toy. He said 'By the sound of it.' "

Cook observed: "Now the only sound made by me while in the closet was simply the rattling of the wheels of the toy as I took it off the shelf." Cook added that the subject was too far away to have heard the sound. He had no way of guessing where the doctor had gone since he was wearing slippers "which made no noise." Furthermore, stated Cook, the subject had never visited his house before and couldn't have known the contents of the closet because he'd been "watched from the moment he crossed the threshold."

Although Cook speculated that this case might be an incidence of thought-reading, he and other experimenters found evidence that some subjects seemed able to pick up physical sensations from the hypnotist. Sir William Barrett, a distinguished English physicist who was as skeptical about the genuineness of the higher phenomena as today's scientists, conducted the following experiment at a friend's country house in 1870.

After hypnotizing a young girl whom he had chosen from a group of village children, he gave her tests to rule out faking. He pricked her with a needle, and even gave her an electric shock, but she showed no sign of feeling. Satisfied, Barrett tightly bandaged her eyes and, standing behind her, put some salt in his mouth.

"Instantly she sputtered and exclaimed, 'What for are you putting salt in my mouth?'" Barrett continued, "Then I tried sugar; she said 'That's better'; asked what it was like, she said, 'Sweet.' Then mustard, pepper, ginger, etc., were tried; each was named, and apparently tasted by the girl when I put them in my own mouth, but when placed in her mouth she seemed to disregard them. Putting my hand over a lighted candle and slightly burning it, the subject, who was still blindfolded and had her back to me, instantly called out her hand was burnt, and showed evident pain. Nor did it make any difference when I repeated these experiments . . . when every one was excluded from the room but myself and the subject."

One of the most extraordinary manifestations of higher phenomena occurred in Providence, Rhode Island, when in 1837 a Doctor George Capron began treating an eighteen-year-old girl named Loraina Brackett. Two and a half years before, Miss Brackett had been hit on the head by a falling iron weight. The accident had severely damaged her nervous system, leaving her blind and subject to spasmodic pain. She was on her way to Perkins Institute for the Blind in Boston when Capron convinced her family to place her under his care.

He magnetized her daily for several months and found that the treatment not only relieved her symptoms, but gave her second sight. When magnetized, Capron observed, "she walked about the house, drank her tea, etc., with as much ease and confidence as she could have done had she been in full possession of her sight."

He began to experiment, taking the precaution of blindfolding her, and discovered she was able to read books and describe pictures which were held against the back of her head. He also conducted a number of carefully controlled and witnessed tests in which she read messages in sealed envelopes and described objects enclosed in boxes.

This is an example of something Soviet scientists have called "skin-sight." As reported in Ostrander and Schroeder's *Psychic Discoveries Behind the Iron Curtain*, beginning in the 1960s the Russians discovered it was possible to teach blind children to perceive colors and printed letters with their hands. Initially, the children distinguished colors by feel. Light blue, for example, was experienced as the smoothest color; yellow was slippery; red, sticky. According to reports, some children eventually progressed to the point where they could "see" things without touching them, even when an object had been placed behind an insulated shield.

Miss Brackett, however, had an even more astonishing talent. She seemed to be able to "pick up" places she had never been to. While sitting in an armchair in Providence, Rhode Island, she mentally visited Washington, D.C., New York City, and even Havana, Cuba. She impressed her listeners with correct descriptions of such minute details as the frieze on a public building or the style of the clothes people were wearing.

During one session, E. L. Frothingham, a Boston banker, invited her to visit his home. She grasped his hands, and took off on a psychic journey. She described soaring through the air on a line with the railroad and arriving a moment later at Boston Station. Frothingham gave her directions to his house, which she entered, finding three women at home. Frothingham testified that "without any leading questions being put to her," she correctly described what the women were wearing, articles of furniture, ornaments, and pictures. "Not the slightest mistake was made," the banker states, "although many attempts were made to deceive her."

The following evening Miss Brackett revisited Frothingham's house, saw his daughter home alone, and proceeded upstairs to the children's room. "After a pause," her host declared, "she stooped over and turned her hand as if turning down the clothes of a bed and said there was a child asleep, but that his head was entirely covered with [bed]clothes. At this she seemed quite disturbed. She said the child was very uncomfortable and that it was not healthy to be so covered up." She then went downstairs and reported that three ladies had just arrived. Two of them she recognized from the night before. The third, she said, was an elderly Quaker lady.

When Frothingham returned home, he found that everything had happened just as she said. His wife had left the house in the charge of their daughter that evening. Upon returning home with the Quaker lady, she had looked in on the sleeping child and had been startled to find his bed covers heaped over his head.

Americans heard about hypnosis long before they actually saw it at work. Benjamin Franklin, as Ambassador to France, served on the Royal Commission of 1778 which condemned Mesmer as a charlatan. In 1784, George Washington received an enthusiastic letter from his friend Lafayette, who had learned the art of animal magnetism in Paris. "I know as much as any conjurer ever did," boasted the Frenchman. "Before I go," he promised Washington, "I will get leave to let you into the secret of Mesmer, which you may depend upon, is a grand philosophical discovery." It was another young Frenchman, Charles Poyen, who later introduced the American public to hypnotism—not as a medical cure, but as a sideshow entertainment. Poyen, an egotistical entrepreneur, had picked up his knowledge of magnetism during a stay in the West Indies, where for years French planters had been experimenting with magnetism on their slaves. In 1856, Poyen and his assistant, Miss Cynthia Gleason, an underpaid textile worker whom he had cured of stomach trouble, began giving demonstrations of the hypnotic art on the Boston stage.

After a lecture full of erudite gobbledygook, Poyen would seat Miss Gleason in a rocking chair and stroke her into a trance. (Some in the audience found this indecent, but Poyen ungallantly declared that Miss Gleason was too old and unattractive for anything but strictly professional touches.) Poyen would then invite members of the audience to come on stage and bellow in his assistant's ear or prick her with pins to prove she was really under his spell.

The show was immensely popular and inspired other impresarios to tour the country with similar routines. Audiences were delighted to see mesmerized volunteers made to crawl on the floor like a dog, kiss broomstick sweethearts, or drink water they were told was rum and reel drunkenly off the stage.

It was one of these traveling exhibitions that first introduced the young Andrew Jackson Davis to hypnotism. Davis, the son of a rum-drinking cobbler who had drifted to Poughkeepsie, New York, in 1838, was destined to be revered as the John the Baptist of spiritualism, the prophet of a new religion. But at seventeen, he was a sickly and nervous youth called "gumpy" by his classmates and "blockhead" by his teacher. Not surprisingly, he avoided school, working off and on as a farm boy or helper in a general store.

In 1843, when an animal magnetism show came to town, Davis was as intrigued with the demonstration as the rest of the

*Andrew Jackson Davis*

villagers, who began practicing the magnetic art on each other. A local tailor named Livingston tried it on Davis with some extraordinary results.

In his first trance, Davis experienced a vision reminiscent of an LSD high. He described an "intense blackness" which gradually diffused until he could see the people in the room. Everyone there seemed enveloped in a brilliant halo of colored light. Presently, their bodies became "transparent as a sheet of glass," and he saw all the organs, each pulsing with its own fireworks of color.

From the brains, crowned with "flames which looked like the breath of diamonds," he observed currents of life flowing through the entire system. "The bones," he rhapsodized, "appeared very dark or brown; the muscles emitted in general a red light; the nerves gave out a soft golden flame; the venous blood a dark, purple light; the arterial blood, a bright livid sheet of fire." His vision expanded, carrying him out on a wave of euphoria into the countryside where he became one with "every fibre of the wild flower, or atom of the mountain violet."

In subsequent sessions with Livingston, Davis continued to enjoy X-ray vision and learned to use it to spot disease in people. He began work as a clairvoyant diagnostician and soon became known as "The Seer of Poughkeepsie." By the time he was nineteen, he had grown confident, handsome, and hairy with a bushy beard along his chin line. (He refused to shave on moral grounds, calling razors an abomination of modern civilization.) Prompted by visions, which now came spontaneously as well as under hypnosis, Davis resolved to dictate a book of mystical revelations. He enlisted the aid of a Dr. Lyon, who hypnotized him regularly for a period of fifteen months. Whatever Davis said during his trances was written down by an official scribe named Reverend William Fishbourgh.

The finished product was a heavy tome with an equally heavy title: *The Principles of Nature, Her Divine Revelations, and a Voice to Mankind.* In eight hundred pages of grandiloquent prose, full of grammatical errors and obscurities, the former school dropout told the story of the universe. "In the beginning," he wrote, "the Univercoelum was one boundless, undefinable, and unimaginable ocean of liquid Fire!" He rambled on and on, describing the evolution of life not only on earth, but on other planets as well. (Martians, he maintained, had half-yellow, half-sooty black faces, while inhabitants of Jupiter walked on all fours and wore clothing made of blue bark.) The final part of his book was a detailed description of life after death in an idyllic place called Summer-Land.

Davis' *Revelations* was a controversial book which immediately became a best-seller. For although Davis challenged the claims of orthodox Christianity, the general public was attracted by his optimistic view of man's spiritual future. Furthermore, readers were fascinated by certain prophetic passages. One of Davis' most sensational predictions was that "ere long" spirits in Summer-Land would open up communication lines to earth and begin conversing with men. Davis promised that "spiritual communion will be established such as is now being enjoyed by the inhabitants of Mars, Jupiter, and Saturn." Only a few months after the book rolled off the press, two young girls in Hydesville, New York, made it look as if the prophecy had come true.

# 2

## Maggie Darling and
## Dear Miss Kate
## on the Seance Circuit

MAGGIE FOX WAS in her early teens when she and her sister Kate, about eleven, moved to Hydesville, New York, in December, 1847. The town was only a handful of modest frame buildings—a schoolhouse, a Methodist church, a few scattered farm houses—which stood surrounded by fields of peppermint on a crossroads thirty miles east of Rochester. John Fox, the girls' father, was a blacksmith by trade and, upon arrival, found his family temporary quarters in a ramshackle, four-room house next to the smithy. He was a dour, tight-lipped man in his sixties, a reformed alcoholic who remained aloof from his family. Mrs. Fox was more sympathetic. A kindly woman also in her sixties, she indulged Maggie and Kate like a grandmother. They were the youngest of her six children and the only ones living at home.

Kate, a delicate-featured girl with gray eyes and jet black hair, was the prettier of the two sisters. Maggie had inherited her mother's heavy jaw, which gave her a stubborn look, but she had commanding dark eyes and a ladylike carriage. They were a high-spirited pair, close to one another, who showed little interest in school work. Most biographers describe them as simple, corn-fed girls who delighted in playing energetic pranks on their rather slow-witted mother.

Not long after the Foxes had settled in their new home, strange noises began keeping them awake at night. Mrs. Fox, candle in hand, would check the shutters or the door latch, but could not discover what caused the eerie knocks and groans. The girls seemed frightened and frequently ended up spending the night in their parents' bedroom. Mr. Fox suspected a neighborly practical joke. His distressed wife cautiously questioned her new friends, but to no avail. Finally, she began to believe the house was haunted. "Some unhappy presence is here," she would mutter. "I feel it."

On the night of March 31, the family retired early, exhausted by a particularly upsetting bout of disturbances the night before.

*The Fox house at Hydesville*

The girls' beds had been moved into their parents' room, and Mrs. Fox had given her daughters strict instructions to lie still and ignore whatever happened. But when the mysterious noises once again broke out, the girls, squirming and giggling in their beds, began to imitate the sounds. Then, to Mrs. Fox's dismay, one of the sisters (some accounts say it was Maggie, others, Kate) suddenly sat up. Jauntily snapping her fingers, she called out, "Here Mr. Split-foot, do as I do!" Immediately she was answered by a volley of staccato raps.

She clapped her hands. "Now, do as I do. Count one, two, three." Three knocks were heard in the room.

Then she held up fingers, and each time the correct number was rapped out. "Only look, Mother," she cried, "it can see as well as hear!"

Although Mrs. Fox, a devout Methodist, must have feared her daughters were talking to the devil, she bravely began to test the invisible rapper. "How many children have I? How old are my children?" she demanded. The answers were knocked out correctly.

The girls were delighted.

"Are you a man that knocks?" persisted their mother.

No answer.

"Are you a spirit? If you are, rap twice." Two decisive raps.

Awed, Mrs. Fox sent her husband to fetch their neighbor, Mrs. Redfield. She arrived in good humor, promising to have "a spree" with the ghost. But after she heard the raps answer personal questions, she ran off to bring more witnesses.

Before long, a dozen spectators were jammed into the stuffy candle-lit bedroom, asking the spirit rapper questions. Gradually they pieced together the spirit's story. It seemed that five years before, a twenty-one-year-old peddler had been murdered in the house by a former tenant. The tenant, declared the rapper, had stabbed his victim in the throat with a butcher knife and had caught the rush of blood in a bowl. Then, after robbing the body of five hundred dollars, he dragged it down a flight of stairs to the cellar where he buried it ten feet deep.

By the following day, the news was widespread. Hundreds of visitors trooped into the Foxes' bedroom to hear the raps beat out, over and over, the grisly details of the alleged crime. "Some," recorded William Duesler, another neighbor, "were so frightened that they did not want to go into the room." Other braver souls noted that the rappings seemed to come from the large bedstead in the room—and that the sounds were particularly strong when one of the girls was under the covers. Duesler, however, found that the noises persisted even when the girls were not in the room.

That afternoon, Duesler cleared the bedroom of all people, including the sisters. He then went down to the cellar with a group of men and asked the spirit to signal if, in fact, a man had been buried there. Instantly he heard a thud like "the falling of a stick" on the floor of the bedroom overhead. "It did not seem to bound at all," he observed. One of the men ran upstairs to investigate, but found no one in that part of the house. Later, perhaps suspecting that a human hand had managed to toss a stick into the room, Duesler experimented, dropping sticks on the floor. But he was unable to reproduce the sound to his satisfaction.

Forty years later, toward the end of what proved to be a very unhappy life, Maggie confessed that the Hydesville rappings had begun as a prank. "We were very mischievous children and sought merely to terrify our dear mother who was a very good woman and easily frightened," she stated. "When we went to bed at night, we used to tie an apple to a string and move the string up and down, causing the apple to bump on the floor, or we would drop the

*Maggie Fox*

apple on the floor, making a strange noise every time it would rebound. Mother listened to this for a time. She would not understand and did not suspect us as being capable of a trick because we were so young." Later, Maggie continued, "There were so many people coming to the house that we were not able to make use of the apple trick except when we were in bed and the room was dark. Even then, we could hardly do it, so the only way was to rap on the bedstead."

Maggie's confession has a certain ring of truth about it, but unfortunately it doesn't explain reliable reports that uncanny noises were heard even when the children were taken out of the house. Nor does it explain the raps' apparently clairvoyant power. Shortly after news of the raps became public, for instance, Eliah Capron, an intelligent and alert observer from Auburn, New York, arrived on the scene. Like his relative in Providence, Capron had experimented with mesmerism. He tested the girls and discovered their raps could correctly answer questions he had written down in his notebook, but had asked only mentally. Several times, he scooped up fistfuls of small lake shells from a basket on the table and asked how many he had taken. When he counted the shells in his hand, he was amazed to find the answer correct. He also claimed that Kate, during a later stay with his family, had produced raps when sound asleep, or even when hypnotized and deep in the trance state.

Read together, Capron's testimony and Maggie's confession suggest that what began as a daring trick later exploded, at least on occasion, into an unnerving reality. While this is guesswork, it might be noted that today it is not uncommon for young people toying with the occult suddenly to become frightened by incidents

*Kate Fox*

they can not explain. But whether or not the girls' joke backfired in this way, it certainly went further than they intended. "So many people came to see us," Maggie recalled, "we ourselves were frightened and for self-preservation forced to keep it up."

No body was ever found in the cellar, although the following July, David Fox, the girls' older brother, dug down to the water level and claimed to have discovered a few teeth, some bones, wisps of reddish hair, and fragments of a bowl. Some concerned citizens went so far as to try to pin the murder on one of the house's former tenants, but they had no success. No peddler, it seemed, had ever been reported missing in Hydesville.

At this point, public interest in the rappings might have petered out. But before the sensation had a chance to die down, Leah Fox, the girls' domineering older sister, descended upon

*Leah Fox*

Hydesville. Leah was thirty-four, plump, and shrewd. At an early age she had married a Mr. Fish, who soon after took off to Illinois, leaving his bride with a baby daughter. Since then, Leah had established herself in Rochester, New York, as a piano teacher. At the time of the rappings, she was living with a young man of twenty-four named Calvin Brown. Four years later she married him as he lay on his deathbed, gaining not a husband, but the respectability of widowhood.

Leah had a keen sense of timing. When she took in the feverish pitch of excitement the spirit raps had triggered, perhaps she recognized her moment of opportunity. In any case, she whisked the girls to Rochester where, according to her autobiography, the disturbances became even more spine tingling. At night the household was plagued by the sounds of heavy footsteps, deathly groans and gurgles, noises of a body being dragged down steps and of clotted blood being poured into a bucket. Moreover, the "spirits" seemed to resent the presence of Leah's skeptical friend, Calvin Brown. They persistently annoyed him by pulling blankets off his bed, playing tug of war with his sheets, beating his bedstead with a can. The campaign climaxed when an iron candlestick, hurled through the dark, split the young bachelor's lip. After that, the "spirits," perhaps feeling they had gone too far, left Calvin alone.

These capers may have made Leah suspicious, but she was excited enough by the game to encourage it. She began inviting groups of guests to hear the girls rap and devised a "spirit telegraph." Slowly she would recite the alphabet, asking the spirits to rap at the right letter. In this way, her circle received its first message from the Great Beyond. "We are all your dear friends and relatives," announced the raps.

The message seems harmless enough, but it staggered the

33

Victorians in the same way a friendly "hello" from an alien solar system would overwhelm us. In Maggie and Kate's day, people were more interested in crossing the barrier of death than in exploring outer space. According to the raps, it was no longer necessary to wait till Judgment Day for a reunion of dead husbands and wives, sons and daughters, brothers and sisters. Now, simply by sitting down with a medium like Maggie or Kate, one could speak with departed loved ones, seek their advice, and hear their replies rapped out.

Of course, in the eyes of the Christian church, this was heresy. The Rochester clergy promptly denounced Kate and Maggie's spirit communiqués as a "vile imposture." Preachers thundered from their pulpits that the girls were clearly "in league with the Evil One." Leah began to lose pupils, her sole means of support, but she refused to give up her spirit circles. She was intrigued by the notion of being the founder of a new cult and farsighted enough to see its moneymaking potential.

The girls improved with practice, and by November, 1849, Leah decided that Maggie was ready to face the public. (Kate was visiting Capron in Auburn, New York, at the time.) Leah hired Corinthian Hall, Rochester's largest public building, and announced that, for a dollar each, citizens could watch Maggie demonstrate her powers before an investigative committee.

On opening night, the hall was packed with a jeering crowd who fully expected to see the girl exposed. However, when the committee finally announced they could detect no trickery, the audience felt cheated. Another committee was formed. This group also failed to explain the raps, and an angry crowd demanded a third investigation. Maggie submitted, weeping bitterly as a hostile group of ladies stripped and searched her for mechanical noisemakers. But once again, the examiners were baffled. The admission of defeat set off a riot in the hall. A barrage of firecrackers exploded, and a troop of boys marched toward the stage, determined to explore Maggie's skirts themselves. A gallant Quaker gentleman stepped forward in her defense and dramatically declared the mob would have to lynch Maggie over his dead body. Finally, a squad of police arrived to break up the meeting and escort the sisters home.

Inspired by this rowdy success, Leah set to work. By the following June, she had installed Maggie and Kate in a luxurious suite of rooms at Barnum's Hotel in New York, where they worked a grueling schedule of seance giving. From ten to twelve A.M., three to five P.M., and eight to ten P.M., the girls held "receptions" at a long table seating thirty people. Frequently they squeezed in private sittings, sometimes before breakfast, in one of the hotel's anterooms where they were properly chaperoned by their mother.

Leah was an astute manager. She arranged, for example, to have a singer promote the girls in a number called "The Rochester Knockings at Barnum's." Business prospered. Their rooms were crowded with excited visitors of every sort, "from the sun-browned Hoosier of the West, to the jewelled aristocracy of New York," as one newspaper put it. Even on a slow day, the girls usually pulled in over a hundred dollars in admission fees.

Leah also worked as a medium. Although it is not certain exactly when she began holding her own seances, somewhere along the way she probably wormed the secret of the raps out of her sisters. But according to Maggie, she lacked talent: "Often when we were giving seances together, I have been ashamed and mortified by the awkward manner in which she would do it. People would observe the effect she made to produce even

35

moderate 'rappings' and then they would look at me in suspicion and surprise. It required every bit of my skill and my best tact to prevent them from going away convinced of the imposture."

This rather catty statement was made toward the end of Maggie's career when she had publicly declared Leah was her "damnable enemy." At the beginning, however, Maggie probably admired her ambitious older sister as much as she resented being under her thumb. In any case, if Leah was at times obvious at the seance table, she was shrewd enough to take a back seat during crucial performances and let Maggie and Kate work their charms.

Horace Greeley, the influential editor of the *New York Tribune*, found the girls beguiling. He visited them repeatedly, witnessed futile searches of their room for mechanical devices, and saw them pass a number of tests devised by scientifically-minded critics. (One of these tests consisted of hiding a sheet of glass under the carpet to interrupt any "electrical vibrations.") Greeley publicly concluded: "Whatever the origin or cause of the 'rappings,' the ladies in whose presence they occur did not make them."

While Greeley was fascinated by the girls' raps, he was skeptical of the messages beat out by the "spirit controls." (Like most mediums, the girls made contact with the spirit world through one particularly friendly spirit who acted as a master of ceremonies at the seance table.) Maggie and Kate's controls included such brilliant spirits as William Shakespeare and Benjamin Franklin. But to Greeley and to many others, their messages were disappointingly commonplace. Take this dispatch received from Ben Franklin's spirit in February, 1850: "Now I am ready my friends. There will be great changes in the nineteenth century. Things that now look dark and mysterious to you will be laid plain before your sight. Mysteries are going to be revealed." But the great doctor testily refused to elaborate. Greeley put up with such amateur fortune-telling in the hope of discovering genuine psychic talent. For every now and then, the girls seemed to have flashes of clairvoyant power.

Evidence of this ability is described by George Ripley, Greeley's chief editorial writer, who later founded the experimental commune Brook Farm. Ripley, along with an impressive group of literary men, attended a private seance with the Fox sisters in early 1850. Initially, Maggie and Kate were paralyzed with stage fright. But with encouragement, their power returned. Ripley reported that "faint sounds began to be heard from under the floor, around the table and in different parts of the room." They increased in loudness and frequency, becoming "so clear and distinct that no one could deny their presence nor trace them to any visible cause."

The sisters began answering questions. Two or three raps meant "yes," and silence meant "no." The raps mysteriously refused to answer the popular poet William Cullen Bryant, but carried on a lengthy dialogue with James Fenimore Cooper, author of *Leatherstocking Tales.*

"Is the person I inquire about a relative?" asked Cooper.

"Yes," came the raps.

"A near relative?"

"Yes."

"A man?"

There was no answer.

"A woman?"

More raps.

In this way, the knockings told Cooper that the person he was asking about was a sister who had been killed fifty years before by being thrown from a horse. Cooper told the company that the raps were correct. While the girls may have been able to read Cooper's mind, it is also likely that they were able to guess the right answers by carefully listening to his tone of voice or watching his face.

Dr. Charles Page of Washington, D.C., found that when he took the trouble to block the girls' view, the raps were muffled and uncertain and came up with the wrong answer five times out of six. He had trouble, however, explaining exactly how they made the raps, which often caused the floor or door panels to vibrate. He finally decided that the girls made the sounds by banging pieces of lead "shaped like a dumb-bell" which they attached to their big toes. He tried this himself and was forced to admit he couldn't understand how the sisters managed to walk about without making a racket.

The most plausible explanation was the "joint snapping" theory advanced by three doctors from Buffalo, New York. After sitting for hours holding Kate's and Maggie's knees, they found that "there were plenty of raps when the knees were not held and none when the hands were applied save once." This particular time, "two or three faint single raps were heard," but the doctor who had been grasping the knees declared that "the motion of the bone was plainly perceptible."

The theory that the girls made the raps by cracking their joints doesn't account for the vibrations which often seemed to accompany the sounds. But one of the doctors, Charles A. Lee, was convinced he was on the right track. He found a gentleman who could make joint raps even louder than the raps made by the Fox sisters. Then he and his rapping assistant embarked on a tour hoping to "blow spiritualism sky-high by our demonstrations." But the new cult was already epidemic. To his great dismay, Dr. Lee discovered that many of his audience, hearing the raps for the first time, became spirit converts. He soon abandoned his project.

38

By 1852, spiritualism had followers in virtually every town and city in the country. Mediumship seemed contagious. Kate's 1848 visit to Auburn, New York, ended up producing at least fifty mediums in the area. After the Fox sisters visited Cincinnati, Ohio, in 1851, a newspaper editor estimated that twelve hundred mediums had sprung up in the city. In the far West, seances were held in isolated log cabins. In New York, spiritualist picnics held on the green meadows of Flushing resembled a miniature version of Woodstock. Hundreds of devotees frolicked "in the near nude," wandered about in trances, sang spiritualist songs, danced wildly with unseen partners, and held mass seances.

There was, however, a darker side to the craze. In 1851, an amateur medium named Almira Bezely received a spirit message predicting that her infant brother would die at a certain time. When he didn't, Almira helped him along into the next world by putting arsenic in his bottle. A number of suicides were reported. John B. Fairbanks, an inventor and editor of the *Scientific American*, became so infatuated with the spirit world that he jumped to his death from a fifth-story window. After a seance with Leah, a man called William Love from Philadelphia also killed himself. Leah had told him that the spirits were anxious to have him in their midst.

While few believers went to such extremes, these incidents give some idea of the powerful influence mediums had on their more sensitive followers. Early in the Fox girls' career, their friend Eliasha Kane, the Arctic explorer, wrote "dear Miss Incomprehensible Kate" a letter deploring the situation.

He began by describing his visit to a well-known Boston medium. Jokingly, he promised to teach the girls a few new tricks. Then in a more serious vein, he continued: "There are some things that I have seen which I think would pain you. Maggie would only

39

*Eliasha Kane*

laugh at them, but it gave me some cause for sadness."

He went on to tell how he had seen an unhappy-looking young man with "a fine forehead and expressive face" seize the medium's hand and beg her to answer a question. "Instantly, she rapped," Kane reported. "His face assumed a positive agony; the rapping continued, the pain increased. I leaned forward, feeling an utter detestation for the woman who could inflict such a torment; but it was too late. A single rap came and he fell in a senseless fit. . . ."

"Now Katie," the explorer warned, "although you and Maggie never go so far as this, circumstances must occur where you have to lacerate the feelings of other people. I know you have a tender heart, but in practice anything hardens us. You do things now which you would have never dreamed of doing years ago and there will come a time when you will be worse than Leah, a hardened woman. . . ." He ended by predicting, "The older you grow, the more difficult it will be to liberate yourself from this thing."

Kane's letter struck a sore spot, but the girls, like the general public, preferred to ignore the dangers of the game. By the 1860s, seances had become fashionable after-dinner entertainment. Celebrity mediums like the burly, aristocratic-mannered Charles J. Colchester, who delighted sitters with his sporting wit, held a number of seances at the White House during the Lincoln administration. Although Lincoln was interested in clairvoyance (it is said that he foresaw his assassination in a dream), he appeared to give little weight to "spirit messages." On the other hand, Mrs. Lincoln, who was suffering from the death of her son Willie, took mediums far more seriously than did her husband.

Although Maggie and Kate enjoyed fame and at least moderate fortune, their private lives were far from happy. When

Maggie met Kane in her suite at Webb's Union Hotel in Philadelphia, it was the beginning of an ill-fated love affair from which she never fully recovered.

Kane, the son of an aristocratic Philadelphia family, was a handsome, slightly built man in his early thirties who radiated intelligence and energy. He had explored the Nile, traveled through Greece on foot, sailed the South Seas, and climbed the Himalayas. In 1850, he had led an expedition to the Arctic to search for the missing explorer Sir John Franklin. Although his mission had been unsuccessful, he returned a popular hero.

In Maggie he found a new challenge. She was, he told her, a "strange mixture of child and woman, of simplicity and cunning, of passionate impulse and extreme self-control." Next to her, his fashionable friends seemed boring. He began to woo her, taking her for carriage rides, sending her romantic bouquets and small gifts—an ermine choker for her throat, a stylish bonnet, a black enamel ring set with a diamond.

He soon fell deeply in love with her, but had second thoughts about marrying a medium. Maggie's profession made her socially unacceptable, as well as, he believed, his moral inferior. "You are not worthy of a permanent regard," he wrote her. "You could never lift yourself *up* to my thoughts and objects; and I could never bring myself *down* to yours." He declared they were sold to different destinies. "Just as you have your wearisome round of money-making, I have my own sad vanities to pursue." "Maggie, darling," he begged, "don't care for me any more."

Initially, Kane, who had a superstitious streak, was as mystified by the rappings as anyone. Later, however, Maggie must have confided her secret to him, for he agonized over the possibility of her "girlish trick" being found out. But he couldn't tear himself away. "I long to look—only to look—at that dear little deceitful mouth of yours," he told her. Although he was afraid she might be lying to him the way she lied to her clients, he decided to raise her up to his level by making a lady out of her. He wrote letters lecturing her on etiquette, dress, and deportment, and ironically signed them "Preacher." When Maggie was captivating the Capitol City, he instructed: "Never venture out in Washington except in the very best company. If you can get a real gentleman, grab him, but have nothing to do with the vulgar members of Congress."

He promised that if she would quit the seance circuit and go to school, he would marry her when he returned from his second Arctic expedition. Maggie accepted his proposal and Kane was elated: "No more wiseacre scientific asses and pop-eyed committees of investigation!" he rejoiced.

After seeing her safely settled in a small private school and telling his "sugar-plum" not to "mope like a sickly cat," he set off for the Arctic with her portrait, which he carried in its frame strapped to his back as he marched across the frozen wastes.

Nearly two and a half years later, in October, 1885, Kane sailed back to New York. Cheering crowds lined the docks, cannons boomed, and church bells pealed throughout the city. Maggie heard the welcoming salute, but received no word from the hero. She collapsed in a state of nerves. He finally showed up at her door and after exchanging teary kisses, he asked her to sign a paper releasing him from their engagement. His family, he explained, was violently opposed to the match. From now on they would be to each other as "brother and sister" only. Maggie signed the document.

Kane, however, kept on seeing her, and some of his ardor returned. When she began to drift back into spirit circles, he objected: "I can't bear the idea of your sitting in the dark, squeezing other people's hands." But two years in the Arctic had made him more tolerant of her failings. "I sometimes feel," he confessed, "that we are not so far removed after all." By the following year, he was more ready to risk his family's disapproval. The night before he left for England on a promotion tour for a book he had written about his expedition, he called Maggie's family together and announced, "Maggie is my wife and I am her husband." The legality of the ceremony was questionable, but Kane promised to make their "marriage" public upon his return.

Maggie never saw him again. The Arctic winters had broken the explorer's health, and he died on the homeward leg of his voyage. For years, Maggie mourned hysterically. She renounced spiritualism and for a while found solace in Catholicism. But her religion was mainly a worship of Kane. In her closet she set his portrait on a black-shrouded altar decked with fresh flowers and candles. At night she would kneel before the shrine, rock with mute sobs, then drink herself to sleep.

Spiritualism agreed no better with Kate. She found life as a medium a constant strain. Not only was she troubled by a guilty conscience and the gnawing fear of exposure, but she was often forced to entertain difficult clients. In 1853, she wrote to Leah from Washington, D.C.: "Last evening a party of fine-looking gentlemen visited our rooms. All but two were as drunk as they could well be. They made mean, low remarks. Imagine, Maggie and me and dear mother before a crowd of drunken senators!"

She was also under pressure to keep improving her act. The public soon became bored with rappings, and in order to compete with other mediums, she was forced to devise more elaborate spirit manifestations: floating tables, disembodied hands, music from the Other World. Although these tricks were performed under cover of darkness, they increased the risk of discovery. Leah, for example, was caught using phosphorus to create "spirit lights." Her followers forgave her, but she suffered acute embarrassment.

Kate played it safer by becoming adept at "spirit writing." In a trance, she would receive dictation from her spirit controls and scribble out the messages in mirror writing. Sometimes she managed to write with both hands at once, producing two different communications.

Gradually she began to buckle under the demands of the profession. She became nervous, depressed and would remain locked in her room for hours with a bottle of brandy. Maggie sometimes kept her company.

When friends learned Kate was drinking, they sent her to take the Swedish Movement Cure in a fashionable New York sanatorium run by a Dr. George Taylor. While she was drying out, she captivated Dr. Taylor and his wife with a series of seances in which they received touching messages from their two dead infants. Kate even materialized "spirit portraits" to show the parents how their babies had grown to childhood in Spirit Land. Once, Mrs. Taylor recorded in her diary, "We kept perfectly still, held both of Kate's hands, and listened in rapture for about three quarters of an hour to music performed in our room by an angel on a harp brought from Paradise."

If mediumship drove Kate to drink, it also gave her a sense of importance, of self-worth, that she couldn't do without. She was addicted to the seance table as she was addicted to alcohol. And although she was never able to overcome either habit, for a time she found comfort in a marriage with a prominent English attorney and spiritualist named Henry Jencken. Whereas spiritualism had been a barrier between Maggie and Eliasha Kane, for Kate and Jencken it was a common bond.

The couple had two sons, and like many mothers, Kate

believed her firstborn was exceptional. She wrote to Leah that she had seen a halo around the baby's head. "It frightened me," she admitted. "I fear he is too pure to live, and I would die without him." Her son survived, but Jencken left her a widow after ten years of marriage. She again took up drinking.

Of the three sisters, Leah was the only one to profit from spiritualism. In 1853, when she was in her mid-forties, she married Daniel Underhill, a wealthy New York businessman. She retired triumphantly from public life, lavishing her indulgent third husband's money on modish wardrobes and costly furnishings for their brownstone townhouse. There, in a salon swathed in velvets and laces, lit by a glass chandelier sporting cranberry glass shades, Leah was hailed as high priestess of spiritualism.

She felt disgraced by her younger sisters, who drunkenly plodded along in commercial parlors. (Maggie, in dire need of money, rejoined Kate at the seance table in 1871. But on the back of her professional cards was the printed statement: "Mrs. Kane makes no claim that messages received through her are of spiritual origin.") By April, 1888, Kate's situation had degenerated to the point where Leah felt justified in having her younger sister arrested for child neglect. Although charges were dropped, the incident left both Kate and Maggie seething with hatred. Maggie, now a morbid little woman in her fifties, launched a spiteful attack on Leah and spiritualism which, she told the press, was nothing but a despicable fraud. When a *New York Herald* reporter asked why she'd stayed with it so long, she burst out:

"Leah, damn her, made me take up with it. My God! I'd poison her!" she sobbed. Then she amended: "No, I wouldn't, but I'd lash her with my tongue."

And lash she did. She claimed that when she and Kate were "innocent children," Leah forced them to become her moneymaking "tools." "I loathe the thing I've been," she confessed. "I would say to Leah when she wanted me to give a seance, 'You are driving me to hell.' Then the next day I would drown my remorse in wine. I was too honest to remain a medium," she sniffed.

"Why," she insisted, "I have explored the unknown as far as humans can. I have gone to the dead so I might get from them some little token. Nothing came of it, nothing, nothing! I have been in graveyards in the dead of night. . . . I have sat alone on a gravestone, that the spirits of those who slept underneath might come to me. Not a thing. No! No!" she exclaimed. "The dead shall not return."

Spiritualism, she declared, was not only a fake but worse, a cover for "shameless goings on." She described a seance she had attended in London that was little more than a peep show. Behind a screen of "luminous paper," a woman swathed only in transparent gauze had appeared to tantalize the sitters. Other seances, Maggie charged, were actually sex clubs where initiates tried to conceive "spiritual children."

On October 21, 1888, Maggie appeared on the stage of New York's Academy of Music. Booed and hissed by spiritualists in the audience, she stepped up to the podium, a small figure primly dressed in black. She put on her glasses and in a trembling voice read a confession stating she had made the raps by cracking her big toe. "I hope God Almighty will forgive me and those who are silly enough to believe in Spiritualism," she concluded piously.

Then, in her stocking feet, she stepped up onto a low pine table. For a few minutes she stood motionless as the vast audience held its breath. Suddenly, a loud distinct rapping echoed throughout the hall. Sometimes the rapping seemed to come from the aisles; other times, from behind the scenes. "It was a weird and ludicrous sight, this black-robed, sharp-faced woman working her big toe," commented one observer. He went on to report: "Mrs. Kane became excited and danced about the stage, clapping her hands while she cried, 'It's a fraud! Spiritualism is a fraud from beginning to end! It's a trick! There's no truth in it!' "

Maggie's performance, with its dramatic touch of madness, was a commercial success, but it failed to shake the beliefs of spiritualists. They dismissed the exposé as a publicity stunt. Maggie, they argued, was a sad, alcoholic old woman who would do anything for money. Henry J. Newton, the president of the New York Spiritualist Society, called the confession a lie. He claimed he had heard her famous rappings even when she was "too drunk to realize what she was doing."

In the end, Maggie gave spiritualists the last word—whatever it was worth. Before she died in 1893, she recanted her confession and once again resumed rapping.

# 3

## The Flying Mr. Home:
## A Sensitive in the Parlor

ON THE NIGHT of March 14, 1855, Mr. and Mrs. Frank L. Burr of Hartford, Connecticut, sat down at their parlor table for a seance. The medium had arrived late, and the rest of the family had given up waiting and gone to bed. The fire had died to a red glow, but a lamp on the table burned steadily, casting a soft circle of light on the three sitters.

As a precaution against cheating, they had each pushed their chairs back from the table. Frank Burr, who had hopes of getting samples of spirit music and handwriting, had placed a guitar, a pad, and a pencil on the floor in the shadow of the table. Otherwise, the room was in its normal condition.

The medium, twenty-two-year-old Daniel Home, had an open, squarish face set with sleepy blue eyes. His curly auburn hair was cropped to a correct length; his thin white hands were carefully manicured. He moved somewhat awkwardly and had a slightly effeminate manner, but the most striking thing about him was an almost bloodless complexion—a sign that he suffered from "consumption," the Victorian term for tuberculosis.

The Burrs had befriended Home three years before during a series of spectacular seances. Burr, an editor of the *Hartford Times*, reported the happenings in his paper.

At one seance, Burr jumped up on a table in broad daylight

and the table rose off the ground, lifting him with it. At another sitting, this time in a darkened room, the newsman took the precaution of holding onto Home's feet when suddenly the medium bounced and soared up to the ceiling on a wave of icy air. At the same moment, Burr heard him gasp like a drowning man. "I knew he was somewhat frightened," Burr reported, "but that all passed off as soon as he was on his feet again."

Although Home was already something of a celebrity in New England, the news that he could fly had made him even more controversial. Now, three years later, on the eve of his departure for a visit to Europe, Home returned to the Burrs for a farewell seance.

The three of them chatted casually about the events of the day as they waited for Home's spirit control to arrive. Presently, loud raps rang out from the center of the table. Mr. Burr translated with an alphabet: The spirit wanted a tablecloth.

Mrs. Burr hurried to fetch one. She smoothed it out on the table under the lamp and pushed her chair back into place. In a moment, something appeared to be sliding around under the cloth. They watched, fascinated. Then the thing "reached out and *shook hands* with the company," Burr declared emphatically. "It felt through the cloth like a hand, but on retaining it for closer inspection, it seemed to evaporate. . . ."

Soon Burr felt the mysterious hand moving up his leg. He peered under the table and saw nothing. Mrs. Burr decided to experiment. She asked the spirit to touch her leg also. But the invisible hand mischievously poked her breast instead.

Next, the guitar on the floor dragged itself over to the doorway and serenaded the circle with a "soft and wild melody." Burr, straining across the table to see, accidently knocked out the lamp. They decided not to risk irritating the spirit by getting up to relight the lamp, but continued in the red glow from the fireplace.

The music became louder. (In the morning, one of the Burrs' houseguests asked about the sounds.) Home was obviously excited by the manifestation and happily declared that nothing like it had happened before. He decided to test the strength of the power. Rising from his chair, he carried the guitar to a corner eleven feet away. The Burrs objected that the spirits would not be able to play so far away from their medium, but Home persisted.

When he sat down again, the guitar drifted up into the air over Mr. Burr's head. "If I did not see this myself," he blustered, "I wouldn't have believed it!" The guitar answered by playfully tapping three times on his shoulder. Burr grabbed it and, holding it over his head, demanded another tune. The instrument obliged.

Later in the seance, Burr saw a lady's slim hand pick up the pad and pencil from the floor and begin to write. Curious, he took hold of the hand. It tugged and jerked to get free, but he stubbornly held on. He noticed that the medium was deathly still. "He was too far back in his chair to reach me without bending forward," stated Burr.

"When the hand found it could not get away," he continued, "it let me examine the fingernails, the joints, the creases. It was a perfect human hand, but as white as snow, and *ended at the wrist*."

Still curious, Burr stuck his forefinger "entirely through the palm" till it came out "an inch or more" on the other side. When he pulled his finger out, the hole closed up like putty, "leaving a visible mark or scar where the wound was."

Then the hand vanished "quick as a lightning flash." Spirit raps wished the sitters a courteous good night, and the seance was over. Afterward, the Burrs examined the spirit's writing and found it was the name, in her own handwriting, of a cousin who had died five years before.

Exactly how Daniel Dunglas Home (pronounced Hume) made furniture fly and spirit hands play guitars is still a riddle. His supporters believed that spirits used him as their instrument to work miracles. His critics accused him of using fake arms, rods, stuffed gloves, trap doors, wires, and music boxes.

If he was a fraud, he certainly was a brilliant one. Unlike ordinary mediums who sat in pitch black rooms, Home often worked in bright light. He also encouraged sitters to hold his hands and feet so they could be sure he wasn't cheating. Men of science failed to expose him, and stage magicians failed to explain how many of his feats could be done through trickery. (One of his more baffling performances consisted of playing the accordion with one hand.) The great Houdini boasted that he could duplicate one of Home's flights. But the magician's assistant quit and the stunt never came off.

Some of Home's more sophisticated sitters attributed the phenomena to electricity—a recent discovery at the time. Others thought he hypnotized his sitters or made them hallucinate. Harry Price, who exposed so many frauds in the course of his career as a psychic investigator, believed that Home was "the greatest physical medium on record."

Generally, physical mediums are considered a class above mental mediums, whose powers are more or less limited to clairvoyance (seeing into the past, present, or future) and telepathy (mind reading). Physical mediums usually have both mental gifts and power over objects. Home often had visions of the future. In 1863, he gazed into a crystal ball and foretold the assassination of Abraham Lincoln—much the same way several of today's mediums claim to have predicted the assassination of John F. Kennedy. Home, however, was largely known for his mind-over-matter talents.

One of the most intriguing aspects of a physical mediumship is the production of spirit hands. Home materialized many hands in many sizes, shapes, and even colors. (At a seance in Massachusetts, he thoughtfully produced a black hand for a Negro servant.)

Spiritualists believed that the hands were made of something they called "ectoplasm," which was supposed to ooze out of the medium's body and solidify into the hands of whichever spirit happened to be present. Researchers tended to turn up their noses at this notion, but in their own laboratories they observed both luminous vapors and fleshy forms coming from mediums' bodies. These they called pseudopods, or false limbs.

In 1923, Dr. Eric J. Dingwall, working with Harry Price, saw an egg-shaped pseudopod in infrared light. It appeared near the foot of the medium Stella Cranshawe and crawled along the floor. He noted that "it was white and where the light was reflected, it appeared opal. To the end nearest the medium was attached a thin white neck like a piece of macaroni." Frequently Price and Dingwall observed Stella's pseudopods moving musical toys which they had placed in an isolation chamber.

To explain phenomena like this, researchers came up with theories which sounded just as fantastic as the spiritualists' ectoplasm idea. Somehow, researchers suggested, physical mediums were able to convert energy into matter. This matter could take whatever form the medium wished: opalescent blobs, long fibers, or various kinds of "hands." According to this theory, Home used his extra hands to knock on tables, play guitars, and even push himself up into the air.

Home himself offered no explanations. Whenever anyone asked him how his powers worked, he simply answered, "I don't know."

D. D. Home was born in Edinburgh, Scotland, in 1833, the same year Maggie Fox was born. His father was an engineer who claimed to have noble blood. His mother was a Scottish highlander who seemed to be gifted with second sight. She frequently foretold the future. When Daniel Home was a baby, he was adopted by his aunt Mary Cook, who had no children of her own. When he was nine, he moved to America with the Cooks. His mother and father and seven brothers and sisters had already settled in Waterford, Connecticut, and the Cooks found a place to live in nearby Norwich.

No one knows why Mrs. Home turned her son over to the Cooks, but he always loved his mother deeply and visited her often. On the other hand, he seemed to dislike his father a great deal. In any case, he flourished as the center of attention in the Cook household.

He was bright, sensitive, and extremely high-strung. Fainting spells and fevers kept him out of school, and he was seldom able to run around outside. He was probably unpopular with boys his own age. Generally, he felt more comfortable with adults.

When he was thirteen, he had his first vision. He had made friends with an older boy named Edwin. The two of them used to go off into the woods together to read the Bible, and one April day as they lay gazing up at the budding trees, Edwin told Daniel a ghost story:

Three days after an English lord died, he appeared to his lady love. She refused to believe her eyes. Irritated by her lack of faith, the spirit reached out and touched her hand. It left an indelible mark, and from that day forward, the lady wore a black ribbon on her wrist to cover the ghostly scar.

Both boys were impressed by the tale. They decided that if God permitted, whichever of them died first would appear to the other on the third day. They sealed the pact by praying together on their Bibles.

In May, Edwin moved to Troy, New York. Toward the end of June, Daniel came home late from a party and went straight to his room. Moonlight streamed in through the windows. He undressed, said his prayers as usual, and was about to crawl under the covers when a dark cloud suddenly invaded his room.

"This surprised me," Home wrote in his autobiography. "I had not seen a cloud in the sky and on looking up I saw the moon still shining, but it was on the other side of darkness."

Then, at the foot of his bed, he saw Edwin. His friend's face looked the same, but it shone with a peculiar light. The only substantial difference Daniel could see was that Edwin's wavy hair had gotten longer. "He looked on me with a smile of ineffable sweetness," Home remembered. The boy ghost pointed upward, made three circles with his hand, and melted away.

The young Home froze on his bed. When he finally found his voice, he yelled for his aunt and told her that Edwin had died three days ago to the hour. "Nonsense," his aunt told him, and she felt his head for fever. But a few days later, a letter arrived with the news that Edwin had in fact died suddenly of "malignant dysentery."

Home's life was fairly peaceful until his mother died. He was seventeen at the time, and both mother and son had had visions warning them of her death. A few months afterward, disturbing things began to happen around the Cooks' house. One afternoon, as Daniel was combing his hair, he saw in the mirror a chair behind him sliding across the room all by itself. Badly frightened, he fled to the woods.

Then, one night loud hammerings behind his bedstead kept him awake. At first he suspected a prank, but as he listened he became convinced that the noises were "not of earth."

The next morning, he came down for breakfast looking pale and tense. His aunt testily asked why he hadn't slept. Before he could open his mouth, a "shower of raps" exploded on the breakfast table. "I stopped almost terror-stricken to hear such sounds," he recalled.

Aunt Mary Cook was horrified. "So you've brought the Devil to my house, have you?" she screamed in anger. Grabbing the nearest chair, she hurled it at her nephew. She missed. Only Daniel's feelings were hurt.

Desperate, Mrs. Cook called in the town's three ministers to pray over her nephew, but his "devil" continued to plague her. When a table jiggled across her drawing room, she tried to stop it by slapping the family Bible down on top of it. But, observed Daniel, the table wobbled on all the merrier, "as if pleased to bear such a burden." As a last resort, Aunt Mary tried sitting on the table. She was outraged when it lifted her clear off the floor.

Meanwhile, Daniel, who had heard about the Fox sisters' rappings, tried to communicate with whatever was making the raps. He used an alphabet, just as Maggie and Kate Fox had, and after some practice received a message from his mother:

"Daniel, fear not, my child. God is with you and who shall be against you?" She promised that if he was a good boy and always told the truth, he would do well in life. She also told him that he had a "glorious mission" to cure the sick and convert doubters. This was comforting news to Daniel.

He began to hold seances in his aunt's parlor. Curious neighbors streamed into the house to hear the spirit raps. They were astonished when Daniel was able to tell them where to find long-lost relatives or misplaced jewelry. Mrs. Cook, however, was certain it was all the work of the devil. She stood the invasion for a week, then exploded. She kicked him out of her house, throwing his Sunday suit out the window after him. He moved in with friends.

By this time the newspapers had spread the word about his talents, and Daniel Home found himself much in demand. He began to travel about New England, often giving as many as six seances a day. He refused to accept money for his work, a fact which spiritualists took as proof of his honesty. Nonetheless, he managed to live very well as a houseguest. His sympathetic manners and readiness to display his gift made him welcome in the best homes.

In Springfield, Massachusetts, Home stayed with the prosperous Elmer family. As his mother's spirit had foretold, he diagnosed and cured a number of sick people. He also dazzled a group of Harvard professors with his floating table. They declared publicly that Home was no fake. The Elmers were thrilled and offered to adopt the young medium, making him heir to their wealth. The Bishop of Hartford's wife also wanted to adopt him. But Home seemed to think he could do better on his own. He politely declined both offers.

He continued giving seance after seance. His sitters saw white flashes of light in dark rooms, felt icy breezes on hot summer nights, and heard the roar of the sea though they were miles from the shore. One of his most impressive feats was tilting a table with a glass of water and a pencil on it. Though the table would lift to an angle of forty-five degrees, the objects would stay put until Home commanded them to roll off. This masterful maneuver seemed to be done without the help of a hand or foot, glue or thread. Home's performances became more polished, but his lungs grew steadily worse.

On occasion, the physical manifestations of Home's mediumship would stop. At one point in his career, his power over objects vanished for a whole year, and Home converted to Catholicism. But the first time it left him, he soon discovered that he could fall into a trance with no trouble at all.

One day at the Elmers', Home suddenly became unconscious in the middle of a conversation with the Reverend S. B. Britten of New York. The medium groaned, then announced, "Hannah Britten is here!" He moaned and muttered and paced the floor like a caged animal. Sometimes he struck his head, sometimes he cried out in pain, "Save them from the pit!" or, "There's no light! Where am I?"

The Elmers were mystified, but the Reverend Britten was shaken. As far as he knew, no one in Massachusetts knew the story of Hannah Britten. When Home came out of the trance, Mr. Britten explained that some twelve years before the medium had been born, Hannah, an extremely sensitive girl, had gone insane worrying about hell. When he had seen her for the last time, she had raved the same way Home had in his trance.

(In a later seance Hannah's spirit spoke again. She told Mr. Britten that after she had died, she had discovered that there really was no hell. Her life now, she said, was "peaceful and beautiful.")

After Home's seance with the Burrs in 1855, he set sail for England in hopes that a change of scene might improve his health. He arrived depressed, alone, and virtually penniless. But within a month, he had established himself in the gaslit salons of London's most fashionable hostesses. His freak power intrigued English nobility, scientists, and artists alike.

While Home was visiting the Rymer family at Ealing, England's most popular poet, Elizabeth Barrett Browning, traveled to see him. She had a taste for the mystical, but her husband, the poet Robert Browning, found spiritualism unappetizing. He went along unwillingly.

The Brownings had a romantic setting for their seance. In the blue summer twilight, they sat around a table in the Rymers' elegant drawing room. Through French doors opening onto the lawn, they could see a crescent moon rising over the garden. Robert Browning watched the proceedings suspiciously, but the frail Elizabeth was enchanted. When a large, snow white hand appeared, Home gallantly commanded it to crown Mrs. Browning with a wreath of clematis which had been lying on the table. The hand did so.

For some unknown reason, the compliment offended Robert Browning. Furious, he jumped up to watch. Later he sputtered and fumed to his friends that Home was an "impudent impostor," a "dung ball," a "spirit-rapping scoundrel." He had no proof, but he charged that the spirit hand was really Home's naked foot or else something attached to it. The poet vented his rage in a two thousand line poem attacking Home as "Mr. Sludge, the Medium."

Home moved on to glittering new circles. In Florence his spirits were strong enough to balance a grand piano in air while the Countess Orsini played a sonata. In Paris, when he performed before Emperor Napoleon III, the dashing young Empress Eugenie was captivated by a hand she recognized as her father's. In a letter to her sister she wrote: "A hand continually touched me and pulled at my skirt. I said, 'Do you love me?' and it showed it did by caressing my fingers."

Home's successes always generated controversy. In England he was constantly attacked in the press. In Italy, the natives whispered that he practiced black magic, a criminal offense. But when the Empress Eugenie installed him at court, Parisian gossips went wild. One of the sinister stories told in the salons concerned a certain Marquis who longed to be reunited with his dead fiancée. Home supposedly promised to arrange it and led the Marquis to an empty bedroom. He left him there alone to face his beloved. But, an hour later, the story goes, the Marquis was found dead with an expression of unspeakable horror in his bulging eyes.

Home's sensational reputation opened many drawing room doors for him, but once he was inside his personal magnetism took over. The Princess Metternich catalogued his attractions: "Fairly tall, slim, well-built, in his dress suit and white tie he looked like a gentleman of the highest social standing, his face attractive in its expression of gentle melancholy. He was very pale with light china-blue eyes—they were not piercing; rather they inclined to be sleepy. . . ."

Lord Adare, a young Irish peer, professed that although Home was inclined to be overemotional and vain, he had a "simple, kindly, humorous, lovable disposition."

Certainly, he had a winning way with pretty seventeen-year-old Alexandrina de Kroll, the daughter of a Russian count and a goddaughter of the late Tsar Nicholas I. Sacha, as she was called for short, was fresh from a French convent school when she met the medium at a party in Rome. It was love at first sight. Or, as Home put it, "A strange impression came over me at once and I knew she was to be my wife."

After twelve days of ardent courtship, Sacha agreed to marry him. She knew next to nothing about his mediumship, and as they sat together on a sofa at their engagement party, she pertly asked her fiance to tell her "all about spirit-rappings." "You know," she teased, "I don't believe in it."

Home drew himself up. "Mademoiselle," he said, "I trust you will ever bear in mind that I have a mission entrusted to me. It is a great and holy one. I can not speak with you about a thing which you have not seen."

Sacha was crushed. Tears welled up in her eyes. She caught Home's hand and apologized with a promise to aid him in his mission.

The young couple spent their engagement in Russia attending a series of splendid fetes given in their honor. Tsar Alexander II sent Home a blinding diamond ring as a token of his approval. Never before had a Russian tsar allowed a commoner to marry into the aristocracy. In this case, the commoner had neither wealth nor health. But the de Kroll family seemed delighted with the match. The wedding took place on August 1, 1858, in an estate chapel outside St. Petersburg. Alexandre Dumas, the swashbuckling author of *The Count of Monte Cristo*, was Home's best man.

During a honeymoon tour of the Crimean coast, the bride had her first introduction to the spirit world. One night the ghost of Home's mother invaded their bedroom. Sacha bravely declared, "She is very beautiful and I am not afraid." Still, Home couldn't help noticing that his wife was "trembling violently" as she lay next to him.

For the most part, Home's powers deserted him during the first year of his marriage. Occasionally raps were heard. Sacha, who was pregnant, complained that the baby inside her jumped with every spirit knock, so seances were temporarily discontinued. Then, on a snowy Russian spring evening in 1859, Gricha Home was born. The proud father saw a "bright starlike light" shining over the baby's cradle. This he took as a sign that his son had inherited his gifts. But later, the spirits informed him that Gricha was only a mental medium.

Home resumed traveling. He took his family to England, where Sacha with her Paris trousseau, her imperial jewels, and pretty manners was a new attraction at the seance table. The young Mr. and Mrs. Home were soon swamped with invitations from admiring lords and ladies.

In August, 1860, an Irish journalist named Robert Bell published a detailed account of a highly successful seance. Here are excerpts describing one of Home's rarer feats—levitation:

Mr. Home was seated next to the window. Through the semi-darkness, his head was visible against the curtains and his hands might be seen in a faint white heap before him.

Presently, he said, in a quiet voice, "My chair is

moving—I am off the ground—don't notice me—talk of something else" or words to that effect.

It was very difficult to restrain the curiosity . . . but we talked, incoherently enough, on some indifferent topic. I was sitting opposite Mr. Home and I saw his hands disappear from the table and his head vanish into the deep shadow. In a moment or two he spoke again. This time his voice was in the air above our heads. He had risen from his chair to a height of four or five feet from the ground. As he ascended higher, he described his position which at first was perpendicular and afterward became horizontal. He said he felt as if he had been turned in the gentlest manner, as a child is turned in the arms of a nurse.

In a moment or two he told us that he was going to pass across the window against the grey silvery light of which he would be visible. We watched in profound stillness and saw his figure pass from one side of the window to the other, feet foremost, lying horizontally in the air. He spoke to us as he passed and told us that he would turn the reverse way and recross the window which he did. . . .

He hovered around the circle for several minutes, and passed, this time perpendicularly over our heads. I heard his voice behind me in the air and felt something light brush my hair. It was his foot. . . .

I placed my hand gently upon it, when he uttered a cry of pain and the foot was withdrawn with a palpable shudder.

Before he came down, Home made a mark on the ceiling to prove he had been there.

The story set all London buzzing. Saints and mystics had been known to fly during religious ecstasies, but Home, a pale, elegant figure wrapped in a fur coat, was an unlikely saint. Critics struggled to explain the incident. One suggested acrobatics and ventriloquism. Another theorized that the medium rode an inflated balloon up to the ceiling.

Home himself didn't seem to know exactly how he did it. He spoke of feeling an "electrical fullness" around his feet, but said he felt no spirit hands supporting him. "I am generally lifted up perpendicularly, my arms frequently become rigid and drawn above my head as if I were grasping the unseen power which slowly raises me from the floor. . . ."

Home's most analyzed flight occurred in December, 1868, at the London apartment of the sporting young Lord Adare. During an after-dinner seance, an entranced Home announced that the spirits were going to whisk him out one third-story window and back in the next. Adare and two other witnesses saw Home leave the darkened room, then heard a window open in the room next door. The accounts differ in some of the details, but the witnesses all agreed that the next thing they saw was Home standing in air outside the window. After a moment he cooly opened the window and slid in feet first.

Frank Podmore, the arch-skeptic of psychic investigators, came up with an ingeniously simple explanation. He suggested that instead of *flying* out and in the windows, Home may have sneaked back into the darkened seance room, past the sitters, and over to the window. Then, by hopping up on the sill, he might have been able to make it *look* as if he were floating in space.

It does seem a bit unlikely that under normal conditions not

64

one of the three sitters would be aware enough to see or hear the medium sneak past them. On the other hand, Adare and the other sitters firmly believed in Home and were probably to some degree emotionally dependent on him. They might well have seen what the medium *wanted them to see,* rather than what actually happened.

Home had been married less than four years when it became clear that Sacha was dying of tuberculosis. (A hundred years ago, doctors had no idea that Home's disease was contagious.) At one seance, the medium went into a trance and saw a "veiled female" hovering near his wife. He announced that the spirit's veil would get shorter and shorter as Sacha got closer to death. When the spirit finally revealed her face, it would mean the end. Home then had a vision of Sacha in Spirit Land: Her flowing hair shimmered with stars, her hands were crossed on her breast, her eyes joyfully gazed heavenward.

Home's vision of death suited the Victorian public. They wept sentimental tears as they followed the progress of the veil in the press. Sacha became a heroine on her deathbed. Lords and ladies came to call and strained to hear her pathetic whispers. At the last moment, the priests attending her heard her cry, "Ah, now I see her!" Everyone agreed that she had died a "beautiful death."

Home grieved, but was comforted by Sacha's spirit, who often came to visit. One night Lord Adare and a friend saw her appear in his London rooms. Home was standing by a window with his right arm outstretched, and ever so slowly Sacha seemed to "sweep down" beside him. "She moved close to Home and kissed him," testified Adare. "She stood beside him against the window, intercepting the light as a solid body. . . . It was too dark, however, to distinguish her features."

Mediums less talented than Home generally found it neces-

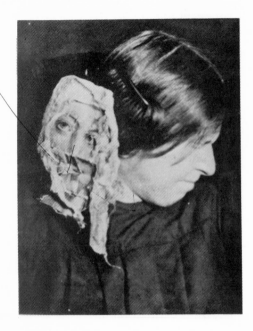

*Eva C. (Marthe Beraud) appears to produce a phantasmic face from her ear in a photograph taken by Baron Schrenck-Notzing (Paris, 1812)*

sary to use a trick cabinet when making spirits appear. When the medium sat inside the cabinet with the door shut, the spirit drifted out. Often the "spirit" proved to be a scantily draped assistant or even the medium in disguise. Some mediums seemed to be able to do extraordinary things with their bodies. In 1912, the medium called Eva C. was photographed with a paper phantasm unfolding out of her right ear. In 1931, laboratory analysis showed that Mrs. Helen Duncan's "spirit babies" were made out of greasy cheese-cloth. She was able to swallow yards of the oiled material before the seance and vomit it up as necessary.

Sacha, however, never appeared in a laboratory. One can only guess about her. Was she a hallucination or an assistant? A paper prop, a giant pseudopod, or a genuine ghost?

It is a little easier to explain the fire-handling and elongation feats that Home added to his standard repertory during the series of seventy-eight seances he gave for Lord Adare. Elongation is the tortuous act of seeming to grow taller at will. Spiritualists thought that the medium's body was being stretched by spirits, but circus contortionists have been known to add inches to their height by stretching apart the bones of the spine with their back muscles.

Home performed elongation in a trance, spread-eagled against a wall. One observer would hold his feet to make sure he wasn't standing on tiptoe. Another would stand by with a pencil to record his progress. Home's spirit control would announce, "Daniel will grow tall," and he would shoot up six inches. He also could shrink himself down to become ten inches shorter than his normal height.

Once, Home elongated and levitated at the same time. As he floated stretched out above the sitters, the top of his head shone like a halo. "He waved his arms," one sitter noted, "and in each hand there came a little globe of fire (to my eyes, blue); the effect was very pretty."

Home carried off his fire-handling performances with no less drama. Impeccably clad in dinner clothes, the entranced medium would kneel down before the fireplace. Then, to the horror of the lords and ladies present, he would bathe his face in the burning coals. H. D. Jencken, the London solicitor who later married Kate Fox, stated: "On withdrawing his face from the flames, I at once examined his hair. Not a fibre was burnt or scorched."

Home also seemed to be able to prevent both objects and other people from getting burned. He wrapped red-hot coals in handkerchiefs or tossed them onto ladies' laps without any sign of scorching. One time, he dropped an ember "about twice the size of an orange" in the hand of the trusting Lord Adare. Adare commented, "I must have held it for half a minute, long enough to have burned my hand fearfully. The coal felt scarcely warm. Home then took it away, laughed, and seemed much pleased."

Sideshow fire jugglers perform incredible-looking tricks by the use of skillful staging and certain chemicals rubbed on the skin. But Home, who sometimes delivered little sermons during his fire-handling performances, told his audience that they were witnessing miracles of faith.

At the age of thirty-eight, Daniel Home retired to private life. He married another wealthy Russian noblewoman and spent the next fifteen years wintering on the French Riviera, where he entertained visitors with tales of his triumphs and showed off the fabulous collection of jewels he had been given during his career. Sometimes he held a seance for old friends. Finally, in 1886, his diseased lungs gave out, and he died at age fifty-three.

The secret of his power died with him. No later medium ever matched his career. Eusapia Palladino (1854–1918), a Neapolitan professional medium, could make a cold breeze blow out from the center of her forehead—something Home never did. But unlike Home, she was caught cheating time after time. The American medium Margery Crandon (1883–1941) was photographed "giving birth" to the "spirit hand" of her dead brother Walter. The pseudopod looked exactly as if someone had carved heaps of animal tissue into crude hands. Home's pseudopods not only made a more graceful entrance into the seance room, but were reported to be perfect facsimiles of human hands. Several of the mediums tested during the nineteen-twenties by Harry Price were able to duplicate some of Home's physical phenomena, but only for a couple years of their lives. Home's career spanned twenty years.

Still, Daniel Home had one great advantage. Unlike later mediums who had to prove their power over matter in laboratories, Home always sat surrounded by admiring friends who, along with the general public, were ready to believe in miracles. While a trusting atmosphere certainly makes it much easier for mediums to cheat, it also seems to make it easier for mediums of genuine talent to produce results. In fact, "good vibrations" from a sympathetic audience will help any performer do better, be he athlete or actor, musician or medium.

Over the past forty years, physical mediumships like D. D. Home's have gone out of fashion. As modern science invented more sophisticated detecting equipment, the great majority of physical mediums were exposed as fakes. The infrared camera, for example, developed for military use, photographs in the dark. With its help, researchers caught many a medium standing in for the spirits. Gradually, the seance-going public lost its faith in spirit hands and floating tables, and physical mediums went out of business.

Occasionally, however, one reads about people who do seem to have mind-over-matter abilities. In August, 1972, *Newsweek* reported that during a parapsychology class at Georgia State University, one student "moved a compass needle, apparently by sheer will power." An article about ESP in the July, 1973, issue of the *Smithsonian* magazine noted that a New York artist named Ingo Swann recently intrigued a group of Stanford University physicists by willing changes in the performance of a "deeply buried, heavily shielded magnetometer," an instrument used to measure magnetic fields.

More spectacular happenings were produced in 1971 by a ten-year-old Negro boy living with elderly foster parents in the rural South. Parapsychological investigator John Palmer of the University of Virginia examined reliable witnesses who reported that in the boy's presence, a kitchen table reared up on its legs, a dishpan full of dishes rose out of the sink and fell on the floor, and a comb floated inside a pickup truck.

Parapsychologists suggest that feats like these are evidence of a mysterious psychic talent over matter called "psychokinesis" or "PK" for short. (The term "ESP" is usually reserved for mental abilities.) Although researchers do not claim to know how PK works, they, like their subjects, reject the theory that spirits are responsible. Today, spirit-seekers must turn to mental mediums.

# 4

# The Reverend Arthur Ford: Psychic in the Pulpit

ON THE AFTERNOON of September 3, 1967, in the studios of Toronto's CFTO-TV, Canadian interviewer Allan Spraggett sat on an island platform surrounded by blinding lights and running cameras. His guest for the videotaped session was a distinguished-looking man with thinning white hair and a prosperous belly. In his impeccably tailored business suit, he might have passed for a stockbroker. He was, however, the Reverend Arthur Ford, America's most celebrated mental medium.

For over forty years, the energetic Ford had evangelized for spiritualism on stages across the world. In private sittings he had won the admiration of such notables as Queen Maud of Norway, the exiled King George II of Greece, muckraking novelist Upton Sinclair, and literary connoisseur of the occult, Aldous Huxley. The most sensational episode in his career had been his 1928 seance with Beatrice Houdini, widow of the great magician. On his deathbed, Houdini, the archenemy of spiritualism, had promised his wife to deliver a coded message if he survived. Although Mrs. Houdini was supposed to be the only person alive who knew what the message was, Ford managed to produce it. Now, at age seventy-one (he looked ten years younger), Ford was making his television debut.

Spraggett, a seasoned observer of the psychic scene who was

later to write Ford's biography, *Arthur Ford, the Man Who Talked with the Dead*, opened with the question, "What is a medium?"

"I'm a kind of transmitter between the living and the dead," explained the congenial Ford. "But I don't believe they're dead. They are much more vibrantly alive, I think, than we are."

Spraggett asked how he communicated with the dead.

"In my particular case," the medium answered, "it requires me to go into what is known as a yoga trance, in which I am completely unconscious and another personality who calls himself Fletcher—and there was such a person, we've checked him out—speaks."

"Fletcher, then," suggested Spraggett, "is a sort of telephone operator who passes on messages through you from people who are dead?"

"That's right," said Ford. "And he's known as a 'control' in psychic circles."

"I see. Now who was this Fletcher?"

"Fletcher is a French-Canadian who was killed in the First World War, and he's been working through me since 1924. That's all I know about him, except that I do know his family (who still live in Quebec), and I did at one time meet Fletcher when I was about five years old."

After more introductory preliminaries, Spraggett called his second guest to the stage and presented the renegade Episcopal Bishop James A. Pike to the cameras. Pike had been in the news recently not only because his liberal religious views had stirred up controversy, but because his son, Jim, Jr., a college dropout and LSD tripper, had shot himself to death the year before. What was not publicly known, however, was the fact that immediately after his son's suicide, Pike had experienced a series of bizarre psychic incidents which disposed him to believe in the possibility of spirit survival.

He appeared on the podium without his clerical collar. Beside the dapper Ford, he looked rumpled: His face was seamed with

*The Reverend Arthur Ford after his televised seance with Bishop James A. Pike in September, 1967*

lines; his gray tweeds needed pressing; his tie was askew. In his hand he held his latest book, *If This Be Heresy.*

Spraggett then invited Ford to hold a seance for the Bishop. Ford agreed to give it a try. As the T.V. crewmen and staff members watched from the floor, Ford pulled out a dark handkerchief from his pocket and blindfolded himself. It was easier, he explained, for him to go into a trance in the dark. He leaned back and began breathing slowly and rhythmically until his body slumped in his chair and his head fell forward on his chest.

In his autobiography, *Nothing So Strange*, Ford gives an inside view of how he slips off into unconsciousness. He declares that the yoga breathing brings on "an indrawing of energy at the solar plexus." This tells him to focus his attention on Fletcher's face. "Gradually," writes Ford, "I feel as if his face presses into my own, at which instant there is a sense of shock, somewhat as if I were passing out."

Spraggett observed that the knockout process took a "very long" two minutes. Finally, the medium raised his head, and in Fletcher's voice, said "Hello." Spraggett noted that the spirit's voice "sounded like Ford's voice with a slight French-Canadian accent superimposed on it." (To Ford, this was only natural since Fletcher, who had no vocal cords of his own, had to rely on the medium's.)

For the next hour, Pike and Spraggett listened as Fletcher-Ford delivered a stream of messages from Pike's dead son, father, and old friends. The spirits said nothing earthshaking. They seemed merely to wander down the byways of the past, picking up and tossing out obscure bits and pieces of information. Nonetheless, Pike was deeply impressed. (For a detailed examination of the messages, see Pike's *The Other Side.*)

When the seance was aired on television later that month, it made international news. Not since the days of the Houdini seance had Ford received so much publicity. Critics accused him of cheating. Pike speculated that Ford may have used ESP to produce the messages. Ford himself, however, stoutly maintained that he had talked with the dead. Exactly what did happen is still open to question.

Arthur Ford was born in Titusville, Florida, in 1897, four years after the death of Maggie Fox. His father, Albert, was a steamboat captain of French descent. His mother, Henrietta, was the granddaughter of a Confederate army captain and the daughter of the local deputy sheriff. Arthur Ford enjoyed a "normal" childhood and youth. In his mother's staunchly Baptist household, there was no sympathy for occult sciences. However, Ford did have an aunt in Jacksonville who was, apparently, a medium. Perhaps he inherited his abilities from her.

Often psychic talent seems to spring up after emotional trauma. Daniel Home, for example, had his first vision after the death of his best friend and his first PK experience after the death of his mother. Ford, at age eleven, suffered the shock of seeing his best friend drown before his eyes. But if the incident stirred up psychic energies in Ford, they remained under the surface for nearly ten years. It wasn't until World War I, when he left his ministerial studies at Transylvania College in Lexington, Kentucky, and enlisted in the army, that he had any out-of-the-ordinary experiences.

At that time, a virus called the Spanish flu was sweeping the United States, killing great numbers of new recruits. Every day the army published lists of men who had died the day before. Ford, who was stationed at Camp Grant, Illinois, suddenly began seeing the names of flu victims in his sleep. In the morning, when he compared these names to the names on the new list, he found his dream had come true. Ford was understandably disconcerted, but held on, hoping his prophetic dreams would go away as mysteriously as they had come. Instead, he began dreaming the names of men killed overseas. When he checked them against casualty lists in the newspapers, he found his dreams were eighty-five percent accurate.

"After a week of this dream business," Ford recalled, "I wanted to go to the chaplain or the doctor, but I was afraid I might be sent to a mental hospital." In desperation, he finally confessed his problem to the Protestant chaplain, but was chided for being silly. It wasn't until after the war was over and he returned to college that he found reassurance from his psychology professor, Elmer Snoddy. Snoddy told him his dreams and visions were not a sign of madness, but of psychic talent. He introduced the young Ford to the field of psychic research and encouraged him to explore his own abilities.

Meanwhile, Ford, a popular member of his college class, finished his theological studies and was ordained a minister. His charisma at the pulpit won him the pastorship of the Christian Church in Barbourville, Kentucky, where he met and married a Southern belle named Sallie Stewart. He was a great success as a preacher, but still felt attracted to the world of the occult. Two years later, in 1924, he left both his church and his wife. Sponsored by an impresario named Dr. Paul Pearson, he began touring New England, where he captivated audiences with a lecture on psychic phenomena called "The Witching Hour."

Based in New York, the headquarters of the American Society for Psychic Research, Ford began watching mediums at work and picking up tips on how to develop his own talent. Gradually he found that when awake, he could bring himself into a semihypnotic state and stand before audiences picking up messages from unseen presences.

Ford's performances were impressive enough to attract large, enthusiastic audiences at Carnegie Hall, but he was still only a beginner. His psychic glimpses were chaotic and random. "I used to wish there were some way to hold back the crowds of discarnates who pressed about," he wrote in his autobiography. "Sometimes I 'saw' them, sometimes I felt them, but either way there were often too many of them. There should be some method, or someone, to keep them in order, to determine precedence. I had to take whomever clamored the loudest, silent though the clamor might be. What was needed was an invisible master of ceremonies."

However, in order to find a spirit M.C., Ford had to learn how to put himself in a deep trance. He began studying with a distinguished Indian guru, Swami Yogananda. Yogananda had come to New York in 1920 to teach meditation classes, but eventually ended up in Encinitas, California, where he built a retreat for his throng of American disciples. When he died in 1953, by his own instructions, his unembalmed body lay in a glass-topped coffin for twenty days before burial. According to the funeral director at Forest Lawn Memorial Park, when the guru was finally buried, his body showed no visible signs of decay. If this posthumous feat is any indication, Yogananda must have had remarkable secrets to teach.

He was friendly toward Ford, but unimpressed with his talent. Psychic power was nothing new to him. He considered it as only one step along the arduous road to awareness. Ford, however, was not prepared to plod along behind the guru. He was too anxious to take flight on psychic wings. Thus, after he had learned how to attain a yoga trance, he struck out on his own.

One day in 1924, Ford finally got off the ground. During one of his trances, Fletcher suddenly appeared and introduced himself as Ford's permanent assistant on the other side.

Spirit controls seem to be standard equipment for mental mediums. Red Indian spirits with names like North Star, White Eagle and Black Hawk were particularly popular with nineteenth-century mediums, although in 1894, the medium Helene Smith claimed her trances were controlled by a Martian who spoke an unearthly language. Mrs. Lenore Piper, the remarkable medium studied by psychologist William James, seemed to be possessed by a Dr. Phinuit, who said he was a medical man from Marseilles but couldn't speak more than a few words of French. Eileen Garrett, one of the great mediums of this century, had her Uvani, an Arab who was supposed to have died a hundred years ago.

There are several possible explanations of the phenomena of trance personalities. One is that both the trance and the controlling personality are simply an act put on by the medium to impress his audience. However, in cases like Ford's, where the trance seems to be genuine, researchers favor the theory that the control is a kind of secondary personality which arises from the medium's own unconscious mind. Spiritualists, on the other hand, believe that the trance controls are actually spirits of the dead.

Arthur Ford maintained that his control was a spirit. In his autobiography, he tells us that Fletcher was actually the spirit's middle name. It seems the spirit wanted his last name kept secret because his Roman Catholic family might be embarrassed by his work with a medium. Ford respected the spirit's wish and never revealed his family name. Nor did he reveal any other verifiable details of Fletcher's life. Thus we have only Ford's word for it that Fletcher once lived on earth.

Ford's credibility is weakened by the fact that he told conflicting stories about his earthly relationship with Fletcher. Often he stated that he had not seen Fletcher since childhood. However, in a 1933 newspaper interview, he declared that Fletcher had been one of his closest friends in college.

Curiously enough, although Ford got his stories crossed when awake, when he was in a trance, he produced a remarkably consistent character. Over a period of forty years, Fletcher never stepped out of his role as a steady, sympathetic helper. Whatever his origin, he was far more predictable than the volatile Ford.

Fletcher generally began a seance by taking stock of his sitters. He would observe where they had come from, what they did for a living, or remark on their appearance. Then he would get down to the business of contacting departed relatives. Sometimes it seemed as if there were a kind of static in the air that made it difficult for Fletcher to hear the spirits announcing their names. "Harry, Henry," Fletcher would lip-read. "No, he shakes his head; ah, it is Harrall." Some spirits helped him along by sending mental pictures of their names. "I see a side of wood," announced Fletcher. "Oh yes, the name is Woodside."

Fletcher also seemed to need reassurance from his sitters that he was on the right track. In his book *Known but Unknown*, Ford quotes from a transcript of a sitting with a man named Schleming:

"Lucy comes to me," declared Fletcher. "It seems she was a friend of yours, a sweetheart—I see you close together. She died in an accident on the thirteenth day of . . . February."

"Thirteenth of January," corrected Schleming.

"It was an automobile accident. You were with her."

"Yes."

"She tells me to tell you she heard you, even though she could not answer. You picked her up and held her in your arms and said,

'It's Bill, Lucy, answer me, just one word!' Isn't that so?"

"Yes, every word."

"She tells me to say she's waiting for you, that though you could not marry, she is your wife and will join you when you come over. She was buried on a little hill in Hackensack."

"A little hill, yes, but in Nyack," Schleming amended.

"I knew it was New Jersey . . . ," declared Fletcher.

Actually, Nyack is in New York. But if, as Ford claimed, no one but Schleming knew the intimate details of Lucy's death, Fletcher deserves a high score in spite of his mistakes.

Not all Fletcher's messages were so melodramatic. Usually the spirits stuck to passing on trivial bits of family gossip, genealogical history, or minor incidents from the sitter's past. Skeptics complained that these tidbits were a waste of time. If the dead survived, they argued, they surely must have more significant things to say. But Ford insisted that it was only through small talk that spirits could prove their identity.

To illustrate his point, he cited an experiment performed earlier in the century by James H. Hyslop, a professor of philosophy at Columbia University in New York. Hyslop set up a telegraph line across the Columbia campus. He sat at one end and posted a number of students at the other. The purpose of the experiment was to determine what kind of communication would allow him to identify beyond a doubt which student was at the other end. One of the students began by tapping out his views on philosophy, but Hyslop was unable to guess who it was. Finally the student sent a message about a streetcar ride he had taken with his professor. "We both tried to pay the fare," telegraphed the student. "Your dime dropped onto the mat." Hyslop promptly identified the student.

Ford spent the years between 1924 and 1927 learning how to

work with Fletcher both in a trance during private seances and wide-awake on the public stage. It was also during this period that he became attracted to Theosophy, a synthetic oriental religion invented by the notorious Helena Petrovna Blavatsky (HPB, for short). Although her disciples considered her a saint, the American Society for Psychical Research pronounced her "one of the most accomplished, interesting, and ingenious impostors in history." A highborn Russian woman who smoked hashish and swore like a trouper, Madame Blavatsky claimed to be in touch, not with conventional spirits, but with Mahatmas, semidivine beings who lived in the remote mountains of Tibet. Before her death in 1891, she had stormed across three continents converting followers with her fake miracles and mystical writings. The Theosophical movement she founded still flourishes today.

In 1926, Ford held a series of seances for Theosophists who were anxious to reach their beloved HPB. Fletcher made contact and relayed a rambling and rather tedious discourse on the nature of "spiritual vibrations." Unfortunately, HPB felt no compulsion to identify herself with trivialities. If she had, the seance might have been spicier. (When alive, for example, she once declared, "I was born with a cigarette of Turkish tobacco in my mouth, and an emerald ring on my left big toe, a small gooseberry bush, moreover, growing out of my navel.")

As it happened, however, the most intriguing aspect of the sittings was Fletcher's own description of the way a medium looks to spirits. They see, he explained, an irresistible circle of light. According to Fletcher, everyone glows a little bit, but a medium shines like a lighthouse. "One can always tell a medium," added Fletcher in his gallicized English, "because the light that is around him is much bluer."

By the late 1920s, Arthur Ford had founded the First Spiritual

Church of New York. His Sunday evening services at Carnegie Hall regularly packed the house, and he felt confident enough of his powers to launch himself on a European tour. In the spring of 1927, he set sail for England, carrying a letter of introduction to England's grand old man of spiritualism, Sir Arthur Conan Doyle.

Doyle, the creator of Sherlock Holmes, was far less discerning than his famous detective when it came to judging psychic phenomena. He tended to accept otherworldly manifestations at face value and when, for example, two English schoolgirls claimed they had seen and photographed gossamer-winged fairies, Doyle found no reason to doubt them. In fact, he defended the girls against skeptics in a little book called *The Coming of the Fairies.*

After Ford arrived in England, friends took him to hear Doyle give a lecture. Just before the lecture, Ford went backstage and introduced himself. Doyle took to the young medium immediately and invited him to share the stage with him that evening. Ford accepted the honor and made a dazzling debut. Standing before the audience wide-awake, he cocked his head to one side, listening, presumably, to Fletcher, and began calling out names of audience members at a fast and furious pace. Doyle recreated the scene in the *Sunday Express*, April 8, 1927:

"Peter Armstrong. Is Peter Armstrong in this hall?" asked Ford.

Doyle noted that a "rather astonished looking" gentleman raised his hand.

"There is a whole group here for you," continued the medium. "Your mother, your sister, Kate, two brothers, Robert and John, and your son, Ned. Do you recognize them?"

"Yes."

"Well, they send greetings and love. Then I get another name, Sarah Edwards. Is she present? Please put up your hand.

Your daughter is here, she says her name is Lucy. You are in trouble, are you not?"

"Yes."

"Well, she says hold on and all will be well. . . ."

And so on. Doyle found the twenty-minute performance "one of the most amazing things which I have seen in my forty-one years' psychic experience."

For years, stage mentalists and magicians have performed similar acts without the help of spirits. Kreskin, for example, a boyish-looking professional mentalist who performs on television, insists there is nothing supernatural about his tricks. He often opens his show by singling out strangers in the audience and telling them their names, where they live, or their present worries. When the baffled subject confirms the information, the audience is suitably impressed.

Allan Spraggett points out that there are many ways of performing this mind-reading act without the use of ESP. He discovered one of the more up-to-date methods while browsing through a magicians' supplies catalogue. The catalogue advertised a variety of miniature electronic bugs which, when placed under the seats in an audience, allow the performer to eavesdrop on conversations before he appears on stage. It is, however, unlikely that Arthur Ford, who performed on the spur of the moment, had the opportunity to rig the show.

Later in the spring of 1927, Ford had a dose of his own medicine when he attended a sitting held by the medium Eileen Garrett. Ford neglects to say whether or not Mrs. Garrett's control, Uvani, was able to see Fletcher, but he does state she was able to contact his father, who had been dead for ten years. His father told him that his mother was planning to remarry. To Ford, the news was a "complete surprise." He canceled the rest of his tour and returned home to discover he was just in time for the wedding. (One can not help wondering why Ford's father chose to reach him through Uvani rather than Fletcher.)

Incidentally, Garrett's most startling seance took place three years later when she sat for investigator Harry Price in London. She had been trying to contact the recently dead Arthur Conan Doyle. Instead, she picked up an urgent message from the captain of a British experimental airship, who had been killed the day before in a crash over France. The captain proceeded to give a lengthy and highly technical explanation of why the airship had crashed. Although news of the catastrophe had appeared in the papers, its causes were still unknown. After an official inquiry had been made, it was found that Mrs. Garrett's statements were not only entirely accurate, but included top secret information about the airship's fuel system.

Although Arthur Ford never produced anything quite so spectacular, he became far better known than the retiring English medium. His superb showmanship, his ready wit, and engaging manners won him enthusiastic audiences across the United States and Europe. By 1937, he had been elected president of the National Association of Spiritualists. In the same year, he married an English widow he had met in New Zealand. He was at the peak of his career.

Beneath the surface, however, Ford was slowly falling to pieces. In 1930, he had been in a car accident which killed his two companions and left him seriously injured. During his recuperation in the hospital, he became addicted to morphine. In the painful aftermath of his withdrawal from the drug, he turned to alcohol, which gradually destroyed both his health and his marriage. In his autobiography, he confesses that he not only began missing lecture dates and suffering blackouts, but felt his psychic powers fade, then disappear altogether for long periods of time. Fletcher, who constantly scolded the medium for his abuses, refused to come when he was drunk.

In 1949, a tormented Ford joined Alcoholics Anonymous and eventually recovered enough to make a successful comeback. He credited the AA with helping him to conquer his habit permanently, but in fact, Ford drank secretly for the rest of his life. Spraggett, in his recently published biography of Ford, notes that although the medium generally appeared perfectly sober, every three months or so he would collapse in a bout with the bottle.

Alcoholism seems to be an occupational hazard for mediums. Spraggett lists a number of mediums, including the Fox sisters, who succumbed to drink and suggests that "personal instability may be the price that has to be paid for mediumship." Certainly Ford, behind his easygoing public self, was a lonely, complex individual. But exactly what drove him to self-destruction is as much of a mystery as his mediumship.

Ford was accused of fraud more than once. In the famous Houdini case, for example, he was charged with getting the magician's message from an earthly informant—a nurse who might have overheard Houdini's last words, or Mrs. Houdini herself. (She had been ill just before the seance and might have babbled the code in a moment of delirium.) At hearings held by the United Spiritualist League of New York, Ford cleared himself of misconduct charges, but we have only his word that he did not cheat against his critics' accusations.

There is no hard scientific evidence to indicate Ford's powers were genuine. The medium avoided scientists, and no brain wave tests were ever performed to prove his trance was the real thing. The only test Ford had while in a trance took place in 1968 when Dr. Edwin Boyle, a Miami heart specialist formerly with NASA, hooked the medium up to an electrocardiograph—a machine that records the activity of the heart. The results of the test were peculiar, but inconclusive. At one point, Ford's heart stopped for a full eight seconds. Dr. Boyle declared he was unable to explain his finding.

The few times Ford was lured into research laboratories his psychic gifts seemed to desert him. During a series of experimental sessions held in 1953 by the American Society for Psychical Research, the entranced Ford was handed a variety of objects and asked to give information about their absent owners. Out of a total of 153 items, Ford had only 26 right answers. By the law of chance alone, he could have been expected to guess 30 objects correctly. This, of course, does not necessarily indicate Ford had no psychic abilities. He may simply have found the laboratory environment a stumbling block.

Even Eileen Garrett, who, in contrast to Ford, almost compulsively turned herself over to investigators, had difficulty when she faced Dr. J. B. Rhine, the pioneering psychologist at Duke University who coined the term "extrasensory perception." Dr. Rhine and his colleagues claimed they could scientifically establish whether or not a person had ESP (telepathic and clairvoyant powers). His tests involved the use of twenty-five cards, each printed with one of five symbols: a star, a square, a cross, a circle, and wavy lines. The cards were shuffled and hidden from view. The subject then tried to guess the order of the pack.

In *Adventures in the Supernormal*, one of Garrett's several memoirs, she confessed she did poorly on the tests. She attributed her low scores to the possibility that it was more difficult to pick up "radiations" from cards than from people—dead or alive. She points out that when the symbols were communicated mentally by another person, her scores rose perceptibly.

Scientists have yet to agree upon what kind of test would provide perfect proof of psychic powers. Although Dr. Rhine's rigorous and straightforward tests are generally considered to be the best available indication that ESP does exist, his work has been criticized because other researchers using the same methods have been unable to reproduce his results. Thus, even if Ford had tested well, his mediumship might still be disputed.

Fletcher's own attitude toward skeptics was "Judge me by what I do, by the messages I bring. That is the only test." In Spraggett's view, Fletcher's most extraordinary message was delivered to Ford's faithful companion Clement Tamburrino. At this particular seance, Fletcher noted that Tamburrino was short on funds. When Tamburrino admitted it, Fletcher instructed him to play number 217 in the numbers game. "Bankroll it heavily," the spirit advised. Tamburrino, not a gambling man, was disconcerted, but decided to invest fifteen dollars on 217. When the numbers were announced, he found he had won a substantial sum of money.

He neglected to say exactly how much he had won, but at the next seance he felt both rich and grateful enough to offer to buy Ford a new coat. Fletcher rejected the proposal, saying that Ford had enough money to buy his own coat. "Furthermore," observed the spirit, "he didn't give you the number, I did."

Certainly the incident appears to be a stunning example of clairvoyance. On the other hand, while researching his book on Ford, Spraggett also found evidence that the medium was not above cheating, at least during his alcoholic period. It seems that Ford may have obtained some of the information he gave Bishop Pike, not from the spirits, but from newspaper obituaries and *Who's Who*. However, as Spraggett points out, the evidence is all circumstantial. There is no way of determining with certainty whether or not Ford used trickery. Nor is there positive proof that he had genuine psychic gifts. He may have been a monumental fraud. He may have been one of the great mediums of our time. The truth probably lies somewhere in between.

Not long after the Pike seance, Ford retired to Miami, Florida. His health shattered, he lived alone, doting on a small dog called Zero. He still held private seances, and one of his last was attended by Apollo 14 astronaut Edgar Mitchell, who was about to walk on the moon. Mitchell was not a believer in spirits, but an interested observer who found Ford "truly amazing." He invited the medium to be his guest at Cape Kennedy for the Apollo launching on January 31, 1971. On January 4, however, Arthur Ford died in the hospital after an agonizingly violent series of heart seizures. His final words, spoken in a low, clear voice, were "God help me."

# 5

## Trips to the Spirit Spheres

WHAT DOES IT FEEL LIKE TO DIE? What is the afterworld like? What does one *do* there? Today's established religions give only vague answers to these age-old questions. Instead, their teachings focus on the best way to live this life. The reverse is true of spiritualism: It is foggy about life on earth, but extraordinarily precise about the next world. Believers can learn everything from what the natives of heaven eat and wear to the peculiarities of celestial fruit trees simply by browsing through a small library of guide books.

These books are produced by mediums who claim to have received their information from a knowledgeable spirit. Generally the spirit dictates his revelations to the medium, who scribbles down the words during a trance. The process is called automatic writing. One of today's most prolific automatic writers is Geraldine Cummins, an Irish woman from Cork. She is not a professional medium, but a self-educated author whose consciously produced works include a number of plays produced at Dublin's famed Abbey Theatre. However, fifteen of her twenty-two published books were written "automatically."

She operates by sitting down, covering her eyes with her left hand, and concentrating on "the thought of stillness," which induces a light trance. Then, involuntarily, the pencil in her right hand begins to move across a pad of paper. She writes exceedingly rapidly, over two thousand words an hour. (When conscious, she is a laborious writer, sometimes taking several days to complete an eight-hundred-word article.) Her pencil never leaves the surface of the page. Nor does she stop to punctuate, dot an *i* or cross a *t*. When a page is filled, a bystander lifts her hand onto a new sheet.

In this way, she produced the well-known messages on the afterlife from the spirit of Frederick Myers, an English classical scholar and psychic researcher who died in 1901. The Myers revelations, a classic work in the genre, often read like science fiction travelogues. He talks, for example, about journeying to Venus and Mars in a body of flame. Other spirits speaking through other mediums tell far less exotic tales. But all succeed in painting a reassuring picture of death.

To begin with, the spirits maintain that the act of dying is neither horrible, nor frightening, nor painful. It is, they say, quite an easy business. For example, in medium Anthony Borgia's *Life in the World Unseen*, the spirit of an aged English clergyman, Monsignor Robert Hugh Benson, describes his own death as a dreamy sensation, a "great urge to rise up." When he gave in to the feeling, he suddenly found himself floating above his bed. He was somewhat startled to notice that no one in the room tried to hold him down, and for a minute or two, he lay in midair, gazing at the ceiling, and wondering what to do next. Then he turned over and saw his physical body "lying lifeless upon its bed."

"But," stated Benson, "Here was I, the *real* I, alive and well. . . . I could still see the room quite clearly around me, but there was a certain mistiness as though it were filled with smoke very evenly distributed. I looked down at myself wondering what I was wearing."

Having half expected to be clad in a diaphanous robe, the Monsignor was both surprised and relieved to find that his spirit was properly dressed in a clerical suit. Presently he was joined by a priestly chum who whisked him off on a tour of his new home.

Benson accepted his death gracefully, but some spirits, particularly those who died violently, seem to have a more difficult time adjusting. During World War I, a medium signing himself W.T.P. received the following communication from a spirit named Thomas Dowling, who said he had been killed by a German shell:

"I have a perfectly clear memory of the whole incident. I was waiting at the corner of the traverse to go on guard. It was a fine evening. I had no special intimation of danger, until I heard the whiz of a shell. There was an explosion somewhere behind me. I crouched down involuntarily, but it was too late. Something struck hard, hard, hard, against my neck. . . ."

Dowling recalls that he fell and, without losing consciousness, "found myself outside myself." Blaming this condition on shell shock, he helped his friends load his body on a stretcher and followed them as they carried it down the trench, first to a medical station, then to a mortuary.

"I stayed near it all that night, watching, but without thoughts," he relates. "I still expected to wake up in my body again." He then fell asleep. "When I woke, my body had disappeared! How I hunted and hunted! . . . Soon I ceased hunting for it. Then the shock came! It came without warning . . . I was dead!"

How does it feel to be dead? Dowling answered, "I simply felt light and free. . . . I am still evidently in a body of some sort, but I can tell you very little about it. It has no interest for me." *

The concept that men have a second, spiritual body goes back to ancient times. The Egyptians called it Ka and depicted it on

---

* Quoted in Arthur Ford's *Life Beyond Death.*

*An Egyptian portrayal of the soul leaving the body*

tomb paintings as a birdlike double of the dead person, which, from time to time, visited the mummified body. In modern times, psychics most often refer to this second body as the "astral body." It is described as an exact replica of the person's physical body and is supposed to be made out of some kind of airy matter. Normally, the astral body lives inside the physical body, joined to it by a long filmy "silver cord." But at the moment of death, the cord is cut and the astral body leaves the physical body forever.

Certain mediums, however, claim to be able to fly out of their physical bodies and travel in their astral bodies without breaking the vital cable. Perhaps the blind Miss Brackett who blithely traveled to Boston as she sat in an armchair in Providence had this talent. Those in the know say that with practice and determination, anyone can have astral adventures, and there are a number of books on the subject which provide do-it-yourself tips. Certainly the possibility of roaming around in an invisible body has a fairy-tale appeal. But firsthand descriptions of the experience sound more terrifying than fun.

In *Projections of the Astral Body*, published in 1929, Sylvan Muldoon, an experienced traveler from the Midwest, tells about his first out-of-the-body experience. He was twelve at the time and "couldn't have cared less" about spiritualism, but had gone along with his mother to a spiritualist camp at Clinton, Iowa, where they stayed in a rooming house along with half a dozen mediums.

One night, Muldoon remembers, he dozed off to sleep for a couple of hours, then slowly awakened in a bewildering and unpleasant condition, "like some queer nightmare in total darkness." He began to vibrate "at a great rate of speed" while something seemed to yank at his head. To his horror, he soon discovered that he was floating above his bed.

"I managed to turn around. There were two of me! I was

beginning to believe myself insane." He noticed that his two identical bodies were connected by an "electriclike cable" which had a "magnetic pull" and made it exceedingly difficult for him to keep his balance. Panicked, he struggled against the pull of the cord to get to his door, but instead of opening it, he miraculously passed right through it.

"Going from one room to another I tried fervently to arouse the sleeping occupants of the house. I clutched at them, tried to shake them, but my hands passed through them as though they were but vapors. I started to cry. I wanted them to see me, but they could not even feel my presence. . . . An automobile passed the house; I could see it and hear it plainly. After a while the clock struck two. . . ."

After fifteen minutes of prowling around the house, the young Muldoon felt strong tugs on his cord. "I began to zig-zag under this force and found presently that I was being pulled backward toward my physical body." Once again, he found himself floating and vibrating over his physical body. Then, suddenly, he plummeted back into it. At the moment of reunion, every muscle in the physical body jerked spasmodically and "a penetrating pain, as if I had been split open from head to foot, shot through me. I was physically alive again, filled with awe, as amazed as fearful, and I had been conscious throughout the entire occurrence."

Most of Muldoon's astral trips were made accidently during a night's sleep, a circumstance which might lead one to conclude they were nothing more than vivid dreams. Recently, however, Robert A. Monroe, a media businessman now living on a Virginia farm, wrote a startling book called *Journeys Out of the Body*. In it, he claims to be able to leave his body at will. Monroe embarked on several astral trips while hooked up to an EEG (brain wave) machine at the University of Virginia Medical School. The tests were sponsored by psychologist Charles T. Tart, who found that Monroe's brain wave patterns closely resembled the patterns of dreaming. But he also found enough discrepancies to suggest that Monroe was at least having a very peculiar sort of dream.

Sometimes, an astral traveler will leave Earth and arrive in another sphere populated with spirits. Monroe, for example, had a close friend named Dr. Gordon, who had died at age seventy. Several months after the doctor's death, Monroe decided to pay his friend a visit. It was an experiment he had never tried before. He feared that it might be dangerous, but one Saturday afternoon, he gathered up his courage. After spending an hour getting himself in the proper "vibrational state," he finally sprung up out of his body, mentally yelling, "I want to see Dr. Gordon."

"Soon," Monroe reports, "all I could see was a blur of motion and feel what seemed like a rush of very thin air. Also I felt a hand under my left elbow. Somebody was helping me get there."

Monroe arrived, somewhat dazed, in a large institutional-looking room where a male voice at his left ear quietly announced, "The doctor will see you in a minute." He noticed that he was not alone in the room. A short, thin man of twenty-two was talking animatedly to several other men. Monroe stood there waiting, expecting his old friend to appear at any moment. He began to grow uncomfortably hot. At one point, the young man interrupted his conversation and stared intently at him for a moment. The heat became unbearable, and Monroe decided to leave.

He returned to his physical body disappointed. But when he reviewed the experience, he realized with a shock that the young man who had stared at him was a "perfect description of what Dr. Gordon would have been at twenty-two instead of seventy."

Cautiously, Monroe states: "This seemed to lend more credence to the experience than anything else. I had expected to see a man of seventy. I didn't recognize him because he was not what I expected. If I had suggested this as a hallucination, I conceivably would have met a seventy-year-old Dr. Gordon."

Later, he paid a visit to Dr. Gordon's widow and asked to see a photograph of his friend as a young man. The widow obliged, and he found the picture was the perfect likeness of the young man he had seen on his trip. "Someday," concluded Monroe, "I will try again to visit Dr. Gordon."

Most spiritualists agree that after an older person dies, his astral body gradually unwrinkles, loses its potbelly, or, if skinny, fleshes out, until it resembles the person in his prime of life. Conversely, when a child dies, its astral body grows to an eternal maturity, without, of course, suffering the indignities of adolescent acne.

Naturally, the existence of an astral body raises the question, "What does it wear?" Although the mystically-minded ignore this problem as unimportant, others have examined the matter in detail. Some say the astral body is dressed in a halo or "aura" of light. Muldoon reassures us, "No one need worry about awakening in the astral and being abashed because he is nude, for his aura surrounds him and no sooner does he begin to think about his clothing than he will discover that his thoughts have already formed or materialized clothing for him."

Muldoon goes on to declare that spirits dress according to custom, wearing whatever styles were popular when they were alive on earth. Thus, one might expect to see the spirit of William Shakespeare clad in full Elizabethan regalia, while the ghostly Martha Washington might appear in hoop skirt and powdered wig.

But according to Andrew Jackson Davis, the most popular fashion in Summer-Land is "a peculiar flowing dress, which, in a moment, can be either wound about the person in graceful folds or

*The "spirits" of two sisters photographed by the English spirit photographer Ada Emma Deane*

taken off. This garment, for either man or woman, is appropriate and beautiful beyond all imitation."

Mind power is the key to existence in many descriptions of Spirit Land. Spirits not only dress themselves merely by thinking about clothes, they propel themselves across the landscape simply by concentrating on their destination. And while most authorities agree that astral bodies don't really need food to survive, it seems that some spirits feel more comfortable on a three-meal-a-day diet. One spirit called F told medium Daniel S. Latchaw that when she woke up to her first day on the ethereal plane, her brother

*These photographs by the controversial Parisian spirit photographer Edouard Buguet show how fashions in spirits change. The phantom below is presumably the shade of Cagliostro.*

thoughtfully ordered coffee, toast, and apricots for her breakfast, and presto, they appeared before her.

Spiritualists generally believe there are many spheres of existence after death, but few mediums pretend to know much about the higher planes. Most of their information is confined to the lower levels. Andrew Jackson Davis saw Summer-Land as a vast garden flooded with crystalline light and surging with pulses of music. The landscape, he maintained, was familiar, but full of "divine significance." Splendid mountains reached up to rolling suns; limpid rivers idled around islands with names like Akropa-namede, Lonalia, and Alium; shining spirits strolled arm in arm along avenues of fruit-laden trees and flowers.

Other less lyrically gifted mediums report that Spirit Land is a neat maze of houses and tidy gardens, streets, hospitals, libraries, churches, and concert halls. In fact, the only difference between their view of Spirit Land and an earthly suburbia seems to be the manner in which the buildings are constructed. Anthony Borgia's Monsignor Benson observed spirit architects and masons line up beside an empty site and begin their task with a prayer to the "Great Creator" for assistance. Instantly, a beam of light shone down on the site, and the workers began to think the building into existence. Gradually, a ghostly 3-D shadow of the building appeared in the light, allowing the architect to see his mistakes and correct them. Then, with more thought power, the edifice became solid.

At this point, one might well wonder what spirits do in Spirit Land. Again, in the more literal accounts, spiritual activities mirror those on earth. Spirits work as gardeners, librarians, teachers, children's nurses, or even scientific researchers. For recreation, spirits go on picnics, visit each other's homes, attend the theater, listen to concerts. While there is no mention of television or movies, an Irish medium named Edith Ellis, writing in 1917, mentioned that there were radios in heaven and that every evening spirits grouped around them to get news of earth. (Apparently Ellis' spirits had not yet mastered the art of tuning in via telepathy.)

Ellis received her communication from a young English nobleman called Brandon, who was killed in the American Revolutionary War. Brandon revealed that the first business of a new arrival is to locate his or her "soul mate"—a spiritual Mr. or Ms. Right. He explained that on earth people often fail to meet their soul mates and end up miserably married to unsuitable partners. But on the astral plane, earthly marriages are dissolved, leaving each spouse free to find his true love. (Of course, if soul mates managed to find each other on earth and get married, then they remain together after death.) Sometimes, Brandon points out, mismatched husbands and wives become jealous and refuse to give each other up, but fortunately, most keep their former partner as a friend.

The way one recognizes his soul mate is by checking out auras. If the aura of an attractive spirit vibrates in unison with one's own, it is True Love. One then proceeds to a celestial cathedral where the union is formalized. Brandon notes that "these weddings are most brilliant when lovers have been united after years of seeking."

What about sex in the afterlife? Brandon avoided the question. In 1917, the subject was pretty much taboo, and Brandon conformed to the etiquette of the time in which he spoke. But by the mid-1960s, attitudes had changed. One of the more interesting sidelights of the communications Bishop Pike received from his suicide son is the youth's frank answer to his father's rather embarrassed query about sex after death.

"Yes, there is sex," replied Jim, Jr. "But not like it is there. It is not physical, of course, but actually there is less limitation. It is more obviously like what sex really means. Here you can actually enter the whole person. It is like you are, in fact, merging—becoming one."

Astral traveler Robert Monroe devotes a whole chapter to "Sex in the Second State." It is, however, a short chapter, for he declares that most of his adventures were "too personal" to discuss. He does report that the merging of astral bodies produces a "giddy electrical-like shock." Furthermore he found that in some parts of the astral plane, sex was a very casual, ordinary expression of friendliness.

In his notes, he describes a trip in which he landed in an outdoor area among a group of seven or eight people:

> They did not appear particularly surprised to see me, and I was cautious as usual. There was some hesitation on their part, as if they did not know how to treat or greet me, but no hostility. Finally, one stepped forward in a friendly manner as if to shake hands. I was about to thrust out my hand when the person moved very close to me, and suddenly, there was a quick, momentary flash of the sex charge. I was surprised and a little shocked. Then, one after the other, each stepped forward, greeted me in this fashion—as simply as a handshake—right down the line of people.

Monroe allows that his experience might have been a Freudian fantasy on his part, and admits there is no way to prove it actually happened.

The preceding glimpses of Spirit Land all suggest that with a few liberating innovations, life goes on pretty much as usual after death. There are only passing references to God. No one ever seems to "meet his Maker," and there is no system of rewards and punishments for acts done on earth. Wayward spirits are simply educated to see what Jim Pike described as a "majestic pattern" of music and color. Jesus, if mentioned at all, is described not as a Savior, but as a moral leader who resides somewhere in the inaccessible higher spheres.

The more mystical spiritualist descriptions of afterlife also reject traditional Christian teaching, but the emphasis is on the inner life of the soul, not the external, astral life. In this kind of communication, the spirit acts as a teacher rather than tour guide. One of the most recently published spirit teachers is a personality called Seth who speaks through the mouth of medium Jane Roberts in upstate New York. (We will meet Seth in a later chapter.) Another spirit teacher called Gwyneth the Life-Giver took control of medium Jean Marshall's hand in 1968 and wrote a slim volume entitled *River of Light.*

Gwyneth teaches that the primary task of spirits is to awaken unaware souls to God. Color plays a large part in this process, for according to the Life-Giver, a spirit's inner development is reflected in the color of his aura. Weak spirits, for example, have gray, cloudy auras. Blue auras signify "love, peace, and tranquility," while white is the color of "pure holiness." The more advanced spirits use their "color vibrations" to heal and strengthen dimly lit new arrivals.

Many mediums mention color as an important indicator of spiritual health, but few agree on exactly what the colors signify. Brandon, through medium Edith Ellis, declared that a pale yellow aura means that a spirit is homesick for earth. But Gwyneth teaches that yellow rays show "an all-abiding desire for service."

Many mediums also claim to be able to see auras around living people. (It is logical to suppose that if the astral body lives inside the physical body, its aura might shine through.) Andrew Jackson Davis, for example, saw dazzling colors emanating from bodies when he was deep in a hypnotic trance. Edgar Cayce, the Sleeping Prophet discussed in the next chapter, regularly saw "blues and greens and reds gently pouring" from the heads and shoulders of people around him. Eileen Garrett, who died in 1970, not only saw other people's auras, but once caught a glimpse of her own. "Within a mood of reverie," she relates in *Many Voices*, "I found myself standing several yards away from my physical self, regarding the exquisite cocoon of colors in which I could observe my own body breathing."

Interestingly enough, the assertion that living bodies have auras is one of the few mediumistic claims which has been verified by scientific research. In 1908, Dr. Walter John Kilner, head of the electrotherapy department at Saint Thomas Hospital in London, England, discovered that when he looked at his patients through a glass screen saturated with a rare coal-tar dye called dicyanin, he saw their bodies surrounded by a cloud of colored radiations.

Kilner speculated that these clouds, or auras, as he called them, were related to the activities of the central nervous system. He found that healthy, intelligent people usually had bluish auras which were sharply outlined and finely grained. Sick people showed tinges of yellow or green in their auras, while dim-witted subjects had hazy drab gray auras. Moreover, the auras appeared to be in constant motion. They flared with energy when a patient was well rested and happy, but faded and shrank with the onset of fatigue or depression.

Kilner spent the last dozen years of his life experimenting and developing a system of diagnosing illness from the aura. The medical profession was distinctly skeptical about his findings, but spiritualists were more sympathetic. Kilner's work seemed to confirm what mediums had known for a long time. One British spiritualist named Harry Boddington followed Kilner's lead and in 1928 invented specially tinted goggles for aura-viewing. These "Aurospecs" are still sold in today's occult emporiums.

However, let the buyer beware. When I asked for a pair in a Washington, D.C., occult bookshop, the salesgirl confessed the store had stopped carrying them. There had been too many complaints that the glasses didn't work. She went on to say that if I was really serious about doing research on auras, I could invest fifty dollars in a set of lenses which as far as she knew produced satisfactory results.

In 1939, Kilner's work on auras was confirmed by a Russian electronics expert named Demyon Davidovich Kirlian, who found he could photograph the aura of a leaf by placing the leaf on photographic paper and sandwiching the two between clamps. When a high frequency electrical generator connected to the clamps was switched on, the leaf radiated a light pattern of turquoise and reddish yellow flares. This "bioluminescence" left its image on the photo paper.

Kirlian went on to invent special optical equipment which allowed him to see auras directly. In *Psychic Discoveries Behind the Iron Curtain*, authors Sheila Ostrander and Lynn Schroeder describe what Kirlian's own hand looked like under his machine:

> The hand itself looked like the Milky Way in a starry sky. Against a background of blue and gold, something was taking place in the hand that looked like a fireworks display. Multicolored flares lit up, then sparks, twinkles,

flashes. . . . In parts of his hand there were little dim clouds. Certain glittering flares meandered along sparkling labyrinths like spaceships traveling to other galaxies.

For a long time the Soviet government ignored Kirlian's spectacular discovery. Russian officials were no more willing to finance research on something that smacked of the occult than Western doctors had been to adopt Kilner's diagnostic methods. It wasn't until the 1960s that the Soviet government finally gave universities and research institutes all over the USSR the go-ahead to investigate Kirlian light patterns.

The most startling development to this research was evidence that the pulsing light patterns were only the fringes of an entire body of energy residing inside the physical body. In experiments with plants, Soviet researchers produced electrophotographs

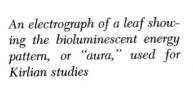
*An electrograph of a leaf showing the bioluminescent energy pattern, or "aura," used for Kirlian studies*

which showed ghostly doubles of leaves. This led some scientists to conclude that all living things, plants, animals, people, have not only a physical body made of atoms and molecules, but also a counterpart body made of energy. They called this energy body the "biological plasma body."

As news of the discovery filtered through to the West, there was much speculation about exactly what the Russians had photographed. Was their "biological plasma body" actually the astral body described by mediums and mystics? It was an exciting possibility, but American experimenters in electrophotography soon became skeptical. Try as they might, they were not able to get any pictures which proved the existence of a second energy body. At Mankind Research Unlimited, a research institute in Washington, D.C., instrumentation specialist Paul Sauvin suggests that the phantom body seen by Soviet scientists is simply a photographic error—a kind of double exposure.

On the other hand, American researchers have successfully and repeatedly produced electrophotographs of "auras." But although the brilliant light patterns have been captured on colored film, no one is yet prepared to explain what they mean or why they exist.

# 6

# Edgar Cayce, the Sleeping Seer

BETWEEN THE TIGHT CLUSTERS of summer cottages that line Atlantic Avenue in Virginia Beach, a bulky, white frame building sits stolidly on a small hill of lawn. An American flag flaps over its terrace, two men in sports shirts carrying briefcases linger by the front steps, a handful of suntanned tourists wander up from the parking lot below. This casual-looking institution is the headquarters of the Association for Research and Enlightenment (the ARE), an organization founded in 1931 to study the psychic work of Edgar Cayce, Virginia Beach's Sleeping Prophet.

Twice a day, for forty-three years before he died in 1945, Edgar Cayce routinely loosened his collar, untied his shoes, and lay down on his study couch. He then dozed off into a trancelike state from which he both telepathically and clairvoyantly diagnosed illness and prescribed cures, remembered past lives and predicted the future. Everything he said during these sessions or "readings," as they are called, was written down verbatim by his stenographer. Today, transcripts of over fourteen thousand Cayce readings form the heart of the ARE. In a small, book-lined room furnished with the varnished tables and chairs of an old-fashioned school library, the typewritten pages draw an international stream of visitors looking for everything from cancer cures to the location of buried treasure.

The headquarters of the Association for Research and Enlightenment in Virginia Beach, Virginia

ARE officials wince at the suggestion that Edgar Cayce was a medium. The word smacks too much of dark goings-on at the seance table. They prefer the title "telepathic clairvoyant." But Cayce was a medium in one sense of the word: when he put himself to sleep, some mysterious source seemed to speak *through* him. The fact that his trance voice was simply a nameless gold mine of information, not a spirit control with a temperament and personality of its own, sets him apart from the garden variety of mediums. Cayce himself offered no explanations about who or what his Information was, but his followers suggest that a Universal Mind was using him as a mouthpiece.

Nonetheless, when Cayce was awake, he occasionally ran into spirits. Once, while teaching Sunday school, he saw a group of Jewish spirits wearing skullcaps and shawls file into the empty seats at the back of the classroom to hear him talk about Elijah, the Old Testament prophet. Another time, on a train from Virginia to Kentucky, he encountered a passenger who turned out to be the spirit of a young man who had died that day. Cayce lent a sympathetic ear as the spirit told his story.

However, unlike the mediums discussed in the previous chapters, Cayce generally discouraged communication with the dead. He believed that spirits (at least the ones who were close enough to earth to get through) didn't know much more after death than they had before. He warned against asking the dead for information and emphasized that a dependence on the dead was as unwholesome as dependence on the living: It could stifle the personal development of both parties.

There is yet another factor which distinguishes Cayce from many of the famous mediums of the past. For men like Daniel Home and Arthur Ford, mediumship appears to have been, in large part, an ego trip. They sought out the spirits, not so much to learn the secrets of existence, but to win powers which elevated them above the common run of humanity. They seemed driven to attain public recognition and high social standing.

Cayce, on the other hand, was a reluctant psychic who took pride in being ordinary. He avoided the limelight, living and working quietly in his Virginia Beach cottage. He fished and gardened, played checkers and Parcheesi with his sons, smoked cigarettes, and read nothing but newspapers and the Bible. In a snapshot on display in the ARE's lobby, he stands in his yard, a middle-aged man in a rumpled suit squinting into the sun. He looks no more imposing than a local druggist, no more severe than a high school Latin teacher.

Edgar Cayce was born on March 18, 1877, on a farm in Kentucky tobacco country. His father, Leslie, a politically ambitious justice of the peace, was a prominent member of a large clan of Cayces scattered throughout Christian County. One biographer records that Edgar was a colicky infant who screamed night and day until an old black woman puffing a corncob pipe appeared at the door and magically cured him by blowing smoke on his feet three times.

He grew up into a skinny, sensitive boy close to his mother and his grandfather, a farmer who reportedly found water for wells by dowsing with a forked hazel rod. The young Edgar roamed the fields with imaginary playmates and, like Daniel Home, often went off to the woods to read the Bible. Although he did poorly in school, he prided himself on having read the Bible twelve times by the time he was twelve.

Shortly after he turned thirteen, he had his first vision. "I had built a little playhouse for myself in the woods on a creek," Cayce reminisces in his official biography, *There Is a River*. "Every afternoon I went there to read my favorite book. One spring day when I was reading the story of Manoah for the thirteenth time, I looked up and saw a woman standing before me.

"I thought it was my mother, come to fetch me home for the chores. Then I saw that she was not my mother and that she had wings on her back. She said to me, 'Your prayers have been answered, little boy. Tell me what it is you want most of all, so that I may give it to you.' I was very frightened, but after a minute I managed to say, 'Most of all I would like to be helpful to other people, especially children.' Then she disappeared."

Like a princeling hero of the Brothers Grimm, Cayce had

made the proper wish. (If he had been the kind of boy who would have asked for a motor bike, it is unlikely he would have had a vision at all.) He began reaping his rewards the very next day. Preoccupied by his vision, he botched a spelling lesson in school and was made to stay after classes to write "cabin" on the blackboard five hundred times. When he arrived home and explained to his parents why he had been late, his father became angry and told him he would not be allowed to go to bed until he had learned his spelling. At eleven o'clock, a sleepy Edgar was still struggling unsuccessfully over his books when a voice whispered, "Sleep, and we may help you." He obediently dozed off, his head on his speller. Upon awakening a few moments later, he found he had a photographic memory of every page.

Cayce's gift kept him from flunking out of school, but gave him no love for learning. After graduation, he went to work first in a bookshop in nearby Hopkinsville, and later as a traveling sales agent for his father's insurance firm. He fell in love with and became engaged to Gertrude Evans, the daughter of a prominent neighboring family. At age twenty-three he lost his voice after taking an accidental overdose of a sedative prescribed for nervous headaches. Able to speak only in a hoarse whisper, he quit his job as a salesman and went to work as an apprentice photographer. In a formal photograph of the period, he appears as a serious-looking young man with a smooth, round face and slicked-back hair who stares out at the camera as aggressively as any college senior.

Not long after Cayce lost his voice, a traveling hypnotist called Hart the Laugh King was engaged at the Hopkinsville Opera House. The town flocked to see him put mesmerized volunteers through the routine indignities of climbing nonexistent ladders, playing hopscotch, and imitating fish. When he ran out of volunteers, he would stand on stage and hypnotize the entire audience by swaying back and forth and droning, "Sleep, sleep, sleep." Afterward, he would walk the aisles and draft those who had succumbed to his suggestion.

When Hart heard from the townspeople that Cayce was suffering from "hysterical aphonia" (loss of voice due to emotional causes), he decided to try and cure him as a publicity stunt. He announced that for $200 he would bring back Cayce's voice. If he failed, it would cost nothing.

The money was raised and Hart, supervised by a local doctor, proceeded to hypnotize Cayce. Although Cayce did speak normally in the trance, when he awoke he was still speechless. Hart left town without the prize money.

The case, however, was written up in the local paper where it attracted the attention of William Giro, a professor of psychology at Southern Kentucky University. Giro was interested enough to consult a well-known New York hypnotist and physician named Dr. John P. Quackenboss. The two men observed that at a certain point in the trance, instead of passively submitting to the hypnotist's will, Cayce seemed to take charge of things himself. They suggested trying a hypnotist who would take a back seat during the session and allow Cayce to take control of his own case.

The only hypnotist in Hopkinsville was a frail, sickly man named Al Layne whose wife ran a millinery shop. Layne, who dabbled in osteopathy as well, was anxious to try the experiment. When Cayce's parents reluctantly gave their consent, a session was held at the Cayce homestead. Layne watched as the young man lay down on the family couch and put himself to sleep, the way he had done over his books. Then in a low soothing voice, Layne suggested that Cayce see his body and describe the trouble in his throat. He also suggested that Cayce speak in a normal voice.

In a few minutes, Cayce cleared his throat and in a normal voice said, "Yes, we can see the body." As his father took notes, he described his problem as a "partial paralysis of the vocal cords, produced by nervous strain." He went on to declare, "This may be removed by suggesting the body increase the circulation to affected parts for a short time."

Layne quietly asked him to increase the flow of blood in his throat. Gradually Cayce's throat became flushed. After twenty minutes, the skin was a violent red. Layne then suggested that Cayce slow down circulation. Slowly the flush faded back to normal. Cayce woke up, coughed, spat blood, and found his voice cured.

Layne was jubilant. He asked Cayce to try and cure his ailments. The next day, Cayce again lay down on the couch, put himself to sleep, and went on to diagnose Layne's trouble and prescribe a remedy.

When he did awake and was shown Layne's transcript of the session, he was decidedly skeptical. The cure was an odd mixture of unorthodox remedies with which Cayce was completely unfamiliar. But the enthusiastic Layne went ahead with the treatment. As he saw his health return, he tried to persuade Cayce to use his gift on others. He assured Cayce that his cures were harmless, but Cayce mistrusted what he said in his sleep. He declared he was afraid of poisoning somebody.

Anxious to forget the whole business, he moved to Bowling Green and took a job in a bookstore. By June 1903, he had saved enough money to marry his patient fiancee and set up a photography studio of his own.

He was not able, however, to ignore his peculiar talent. Periodically he would again lose his voice and resort to Layne for help. Friends and relatives asked and received help where doctors had failed. His startling successes aroused the interest of medical men, and Cayce held experimental sessions for them until one unbelieving doctor tested Cayce's trance by sticking his penknife under Cayce's fingernail. Cayce awoke in pain, angrily swearing that he would never again be a scientist's guinea pig. He continued, however, giving health readings for friends. Word of his gift spread. By 1910, he was interrupting work in his photography studio to give two readings a day.

Cayce had no memory of what occurred during his trances. The transcripts of his readings indicate that he actually saw the patient's body, but it is not known whether, like Andrew Jackson Davis, he could peer through bodies and examine organs swirling with colors. In any case, unlike Davis and other clairvoyant healers, Cayce was able to diagnose at a distance. When he went into a trance, his assistant would simply read the name and address of a patient in another part of town, or even another state. By Cayce's own wish, no other information was given. After a few moments, Cayce would announce, "Yes, we have the body." Then he would begin to list the patient's symptoms. Sometimes he would mention what sort of pajamas the patient was wearing or comment on a picture hanging on the bedroom wall. To observers it seemed as if Cayce was paying a house call.

At this time, Cayce's hypnotist was an enterprising homeopathic doctor named Wesley H. Ketchum. Ketchum won Cayce national notoriety by publicizing his talent in newspapers across the country. The October 9, 1910, edition of the *New York Times* ran a story headlined, "Illiterate man becomes doctor when hypnotized." Soon Cayce was deluged with letters from across the world. Missionaries in Turkey and India asked for his help, as did a United States senator and a Hollywood actress. Once, petitioned

*Edgar Cayce*

by a member of Italian royalty, Cayce began his reading in fluent Italian.

Cayce himself, however, still lacked faith in his readings. When his second son came down with whooping cough, he relied on doctors, not his Information, and the baby died. When his wife Gertrude appeared to be dying of tuberculosis, it was only as a last resort that he consented to give a reading for her. From his sleep he prescribed doses of heroin and recommended that she breathe in fumes from a warm keg of apple brandy. The treatment was carried out, and gradually his wife recovered.

If he had any lingering doubts about the efficacy of his cures, they were dispelled in 1914 when his oldest son, toddler Hugh Lynn, lit a match to a pile of photographic powder and burned his eyes. Specialists, who maintained there was no hope for the boy's sight, told Cayce they would have to operate and remove one eye in order to save his son's life.

Cayce, however, decided to consult his Information. The reading announced that Hugh Lynn's sight was not beyond repair and instructed Cayce to soak bandages with tannic acid and apply them to the boy's eyes for fifteen days. The doctors protested that tannic acid was too strong for the eyes, but since they believed Hugh Lynn's sight was already destroyed, their objections were academic. Cayce proceeded with the treatment, and on the sixteenth day, when the bandages were removed, a white mass sloughed off with the dressings and Hugh Lynn declared that he could see.

There are many people alive today, including Hugh Lynn, who will testify that Cayce's readings helped cure everything from arthritis to cancer. In some instances these claims are supported by medical evidence. There are, however, no records to show exactly how often Cayce's remedies worked. Enthusiasts declare that Cayce was infallible *if* his treatments were properly carried out. But the "if" is a big one: Cayce's prescriptions were complex, time-consuming disciplines for both body and soul. They included medicines that were difficult to obtain, peculiar diets, exercises, prayer, and meditation. Numbers of sufferers lost patience and either ignored one aspect of the cure or abandoned it altogether. Many found it easier to bear their diseases than to follow Cayce's remedies.

Although the majority of Cayce's readings were given for

people with medical problems, Cayce occasionally used his trance Information for financial purposes. After World War I, for example, when Cayce was trying to raise money to build a hospital for carrying out his treatments, he went to Texas in search of oil. His readings located a well, but after months of unsuccessful drilling, he gave up. He believed his Information had failed because his partners were more interested in striking it rich than in building a hospital.

Cayce's readings took on still another dimension when, in 1923, he met Arthur Lammers, a wealthy printer from Dayton, Ohio, who made a hobby of studying mystical philosophies. Having delved into the mystery religions of ancient Egypt and Greece, yoga, medieval alchemy, and astrology, he came to Cayce, not for a health reading, but to find out the truth about man's existence on earth. It was a novel request, and Cayce agreed to a session.

Lammers began by asking for his horoscope and got more than he had bargained for. The sleeping Cayce not only told him what influence the stars and planets had on his present life, but described their effect on former lives, including one incarnation as a medieval monk. According to Cayce's Information, all men are born and die, not once, but many times.

When he awoke, the Bible-loving Cayce was shocked to find his Information affirming the Hindu concept of reincarnation. Nonetheless, he continued his sessions with Lammers. His readings supported the Eastern belief that each man is subject to the law of karma—a Sanskrit word meaning "act" or "deed." Basically, the law of karma is the law of cause and effect: Whatever a person does, be it good or bad, determines his fate not only from day to day, but from life to life. Thus, a mother might pay for neglecting her children by ending up as an unwanted old woman. In the same way, a crippled man might be rewarded for virtuous acts by being reborn with the body of an athlete.

Cayce gradually came to accept reincarnation. It not only made life's injustices seem more tolerable, but it helped explain people's inner drives and directions. In his own case, for example, the readings told him he had once attained great spiritual heights as a priest in Egypt but had regressed by wallowing in luxuries and running off with the daughter of a fellow priest. From his Egyptian life, the readings pointed out, Cayce inherited not only a strong pull toward fleshly comforts, but the girl as well. She was presently reincarnated as his wife Gertrude.

Again, the readings told him that his psychic abilities derived from a life in ancient Persia when, as a leader, he had been mortally wounded in a raid and lay dying alone on a plain. In an effort to overcome his excruciating pain, he succeeded in separating his mind from his body, a feat which led to the development of his psychic talents.

Cayce's Christian faith was also described as a carry-over from a former life. As a soldier of fortune named Lucius of Cyrene, he had joined Jesus' followers after the crucifixion. (Incidentally, the readings suggested that Jesus himself taught reincarnation when he told his disciples, "Unless a man be reborn, he shall not enter the Kingdom of Heaven.")

According to the readings, Cayce slipped down the ladder of moral progress in his most recent incarnation as an early American drifter named John Bainbridge. He was not only a seducer of women (including one Indian maid who thereafter mistrusted all white men), but a gambler who misused his psychic gift to win fortune. Eventually, Bainbridge perished fleeing from Indians down the Ohio River on a raft. He was reborn as Edgar Cayce and given a chance to atone for the past by helping others with his readings.

Thus, in addition to his health readings, Cayce began giving "life readings." He hoped to help people improve their lives by making them aware of past sins and successes, of inherited talents and traits. In one life reading, for example, he told a sixteen-year-old girl that she had been an artist in Ancient Greece. He suggested that she would make a fine wallpaper designer and urged, "Keep *self* unspotted, but be not sulky in doing so!" Another reading revealed that an eleven-year-old boy had lived before as an English intelligence officer during the American Revolution. From this incarnation the boy had inherited a bossy manner and the habit of leaving his room in a mess. (As an officer he had had a valet to pick up after him.)

Cayce's readings stressed self-reliance. A young man came to Cayce for career advice and was told he would be successful in almost any line of work. Unsatisfied, the young man demanded to know what job to choose. "Whether it's shoeing horses or digging ditches," came the reply, "*choose!* And then do it!" Again, the young man asked which way to turn. Cayce sharply told him to turn to himself.

Although the young man went on to become first a motorcycle policeman and later a respected parole officer, throughout his life he appeared to depend on Cayce more than on himself. Perhaps his wife, a high-strung invalid, resented this. It seems she occasionally tried to rival Cayce by giving readings of her own.

Many of Cayce's life readings went back thirty thousand years, long before the Stone Age. At that time, his Information revealed, a vast continent called Atlantis existed in the Atlantic Ocean. The level of civilization on Atlantis was highly advanced. Men not only enjoyed telephones and television, but they had managed to harness the energy of the sun by constructing giant laserlike crystals for power plants. (At the time Cayce spoke, lasers had not yet been discovered.) These crystals, or Firestones, as Cayce called them, transmitted invisible beams which powered remote-controlled cars, aircraft, and submarines. Like atomic energy, the Firestones also had a destructive side, and the Atlanteans once used them as death rays to exterminate hordes of huge beasts overrunning the earth.

According to Cayce's readings, the crystals were guarded by a priestly class of citizens dedicated to the common good. In time, however, a more selfish group took control. Through their carelessness, the energy level of the Firestones was turned up too high. In a cataclysmic explosion, Atlantis broke up into islands and gradually sunk into the sea. Cayce believed that a large number of Atlanteans are being reborn today, because our technology offers them an appropriate opportunity to correct their past blunders.

Cayce predicted in 1944 that the world would have proof of the lost continent's existence by the late 1960s when one of the larger islands would begin to surface off the coast of Florida. While in recent years a number of underwater explorers claim to have turned up evidences of an unknown ancient civilization in Bahamian waters, none of the supposed discoveries has been verified by scientists. Even the ARE hesitates to accept the findings as proof of Cayce's prophecy.

Edgar Cayce is far more popular today than he was in his own lifetime. His homey health recommendations (three almonds a day keep cancer away, for example), his teachings on dreams and reincarnation, his acceptance of astrology all have a timely appeal for Aquarian adventurers. ARE study groups can be found in cities, towns, and even prisons from Alaska to Florida. Not surprisingly, Cayce has strongly influenced practicing psychics. As can be seen in the next chapters, the more sophisticated mediums are now more likely to talk about former lives and self-determination than to bring greetings from relatives in the Great Beyond.

# 7

# Life after Life after Life

AS DESCRIBED by Edgar Cayce, reincarnation seems to be as automatic a process as the change of seasons. Individuals keep on being reborn until they have worked out their destiny, or karma. The cycle is an immutable fact of the afterlife.

Other mediums, however, have expressed a different view. Geraldine Cummins, the automatic writer who earlier this century communicated with the spirit of Frederick Myers, reveals that reincarnation is by no means obligatory, but a matter of personal choice. Myers explains that it is not necessary to return to earth to learn all the varieties of human experience. He believes one can absorb them by "entering into the experience of other departed souls." On the other hand, he confesses that his beliefs "can not, by any means, be said to be the last word on the subject."

More recently, the element of choice in reincarnation has been stressed in the writings of medium Jane Roberts who lives in Elmira, New York. Roberts, a professional writer who has published short stories and a novel, first became aware of her psychic abilities in 1963 when she began experimenting with a Ouija board for a book she was writing on ESP. Initially, a personality named Seth began spelling out messages on the board. Then, after a couple weeks' practice, Roberts began hearing his words in her head. Eventually, she began speaking for him during a trance. Her husband, an artist, wrote down the communications, which she has published in two volumes, *Seth Material* and *Seth Speaks*.

Seth calls himself an "energy essence." He insists that he is neither "some degenerating secondary personality of Rubert's" (Jane Roberts' name in a former incarnation), nor "some long-bearded, beady-eyed spirit sitting on cloud nine." While he does admit that he had lived before on earth, he also claims to be part of a more highly evolved consciousness. But whatever else Seth may be, over the last ten years, he has been acting as a teacher.

*A Ouija board advertised in a 1944 issue of* The Occult

Occasionally he arrives to take over one of Jane Roberts' own ESP classes. Her voice, her facial expressions, her gestures become masculine and uncharacteristically professorial as he speaks through her to a mixed group of students: men in business suits, housewives, youths in jeans and beads who sit cross-legged on the floor. As the students sip wine, Seth, like Cayce's Information, expounds on the nature of reality, keys to health, reincarnation, and ancient civilizations. (Seth maintains that three highly developed civilizations preceded Atlantis. In *Seth Speaks* he describes the second one, Lumania, in detail. The Lumanians, it seems, were a physically weak, highly intelligent race whose pacificism led to their downfall.)

Unlike Cayce's Information, however, Seth's syntax and presentation are remarkably clear and precise. He also lightens up the sessions with his sense of humor. Take the following exchange in *Seth Speaks:*

> Student: "Have you always taught on reincarnation?"
>
> Seth: "Teaching has been my main object, but I have not always been a teacher. I was a spice merchant at one time. A round and fat and heavy spice merchant."
>
> Student: "But handsome."
>
> Seth, with a smile: "I do not know what to do with you. We learned what spices would do long before the present generation got hung-up on grass. We got high on the high seas sniffing oregano."

Seth's reincarnation teachings emphasize free choice. In between lives, souls rest, take stock of the past, and plan the future. They decide whether to be reborn as male or female and whether to incarnate with friends and family from past lives or to go it alone. They also choose whether to develop one side of the personality at a time or to work more gradually with the whole self.

Misfortune and illness, Seth insists, are not punishments but personal choices. To illustrate this, Roberts cites the case of "Sally," a young woman in her twenties stricken with multiple sclerosis. When her distraught husband brought her to a Seth session, she was going blind and was unable to speak or move at will. Doctors had given her a year to live.

Seth explained that in the recent past she had lived as Nicolo, a widower in an Italian hilltown. He lived with his daughter Rosalina, a highly neurotic cripple. Although he cared for her well, he resented her greatly, for she made it impossible for him to remarry. It happened that Rosalina, a good-looking woman in spite of her handicap, eventually eloped with a farmhand. Nicolo-Sally became lonely and embittered. He was now too old to attract a wife.

For his next reincarnation, Nicolo-Sally chose a happier life and was reborn as the wife of a wealthy landowner in a neighboring district. But after that experience, he decided to grow further by stepping into his daughter's shoes. He wanted to learn what it felt like to be totally dependent on someone and courageously took on a critical disease.

Two years after this reading, as Sally lay in a coma near death, Seth told her husband that she had learned the lesson she had set up for herself. In doing so, however, she had damaged her body beyond repair and had decided to leave it. Now, Seth declared, she was rearranging "the furniture of her mind" for another life.

According to Seth, individuals keep on being reborn until

they are ready to enter "other dimensions of reality." (He is not explicit about what the other realities are like.) However, before a person can leave the earth plane, he must have experienced at least three roles: mother, father, and child. Ambitious souls can fulfill this minimum requirement in only two lives.

Perhaps the most startling and difficult to understand aspect of Seth's teaching is his theory that people actually live all their lives at once. Time, he maintains, is illusion, and although it is convenient to think of past lives strung out one after the other, in fact, everything exists simultaneously. "You and your reincarnated selves, or personalities, are not imprisoned in time," he instructs. "There is a constant interchange going on between what you think of as your present self and your past and future selves." And again he insists: "You are not imprisoned in time unless you believe that you are, and there is nothing more important than belief."

In her book, *How to Develop Your ESP Power*, Jane Roberts suggests that the ordinary person may be able to get some insight into his or her former lives through hypnosis. In the famous Bridey Murphy case in the 1950s a Boston housewife under the influence of hypnosis began "remembering" a past life in nineteenth-century Ireland. A similar case occurred more recently in 1962 when a Canadian teenager named Joanne MacIver was taken back in time by her father, an amateur hypnotist. During hypnosis she claimed to have lived before as "Susanne Ganier," an eighteenth-century farmer's wife in Northern Ontario. (The evidence of the case is examined in Jess Stearn's *The Girl with the Blue Eyes*.)

Often subjects who have undergone hypnotic regression end up believing that they have indeed lived before. Although they have no objective proof, the trance material has a personal ring of truth for them. Scientists, however, generally dismiss these cases as examples of subconscious role-playing. They declare that the "memories" unearthed during hypnosis are simply fantasies.

Nonetheless, a few pioneering scientists take the possibility of reincarnation seriously. In their search for proof they turn not to instances of hypnotic regression, but to cases in which people suddenly, for no apparent reason, become conscious of a former life. In this country, the man at the forefront of reincarnational research is Dr. Ian Stevenson, an eminent psychiatrist and parapsychologist at the University of Virginia School of Medicine. Dr. Stevenson has investigated hundreds of people claiming to remember past existences. Most of his cases have involved young children, who eventually grew up into ordinary, sane adults. He has found that surprisingly few of the cases are explainable by fantasy or fraud. (Only 5 percent of 300 cases have collapsed under his scrutiny.)

In his prize-winning work *Twenty Cases Suggestive of Reincarnation*, he discusses his investigation of a boy in India named Ravi Shankar (no relation to the famed musician). In January, 1951, in a city in the Chipatti District of Kanauj, a six-year-old boy named Munna, the only son of a barber, was enticed away from his play by two neighbors and brutally murdered with a razor. It appears that one of the men was a relative who stood to inherit money if Munna was out of the way. The men were arrested, but escaped conviction as there were no witnesses to the crime.

Six months later, in July, 1951, Ravi was born in another part of the city, half a mile away from Munna's house. Between the ages of two and three, Ravi began asking for toys he said he had had in his previous life. His name, he said, had been Munna. He often talked about the way he died: he had been beheaded by two hoodlums. On his throat he had a long birthmark which resembled a scar. (The mark faded as he grew older.)

When Munna's father heard about Ravi, he came to visit. After hearing Ravi, then four years old, describe Munna's house, toys, and relatives in detail, Munna's father became convinced that Ravi was his son reborn. Ravi's father, however, became fearful that his son might be taken from him and beat the boy to make him stop "remembering."

Stevenson visited Ravi and his family in 1964. Using his psychiatric skills to rule out fraud, he concluded that Ravi did, in fact, possess intimate knowledge of Munna's life and that he probably did not obtain it in a normal way. Stevenson cautiously points out that Ravi's uncanny memories are not necessarily a proof of reincarnation. The boy may have been able to tune in to Munna's life in some superpsychic way. Stevenson believes that birthmarks, like the one Ravi had on his throat, can provide stronger evidence for reincarnation than memories.

Again in *Twenty Cases*, Stevenson cites the case of Corliss Chotkin, a part Tlingit Indian, part Anglo-Saxon, living in Alaska. According to Tlingit tradition, tribesmen are not only reborn, but can choose their next parents. In 1946, a full-blooded Tlingit named Victor Vincent told his niece, "I am coming back after I die as your son. Your son will have these scars." He pointed to a scar on the right side of his nose and to one on his back. Both scars were the result of surgery.

Eighteen months after Victor's death, his niece gave birth to a son who had two peculiar-looking birthmarks, one on the right side of his nose, the other on his back. She named the boy Corliss. When Corliss was thirteen months old, one day he suddenly declared, "Don't you know me? I'm Kahkody." Kahkody was Victor's tribal name. Thenceforth Corliss began to show the same personality traits as his dead uncle. He also correctly related incidents from Victor Vincent's life which his parents knew nothing about.

Stevenson made three visits to Alaska to investigate. He photographed Corliss' birthmarks and noted their dramatic resemblance to surgical scars. The one on Corliss' back even had stitch marks. In Stevenson's opinion, it is asking too much to chalk up the marks to coincidence. He thinks it likely that Victor Vincent had been reborn as Corliss. (Incidentally, at age nine, Corliss' memories of his past life began to fade. When Stevenson visited him at fifteen, he said he remembered nothing.)

Stevenson emphasizes that none of his cases are flawless. Corliss' birthmarks, for example, may not have been made by Victor Vincent. His mother may have had the psychokinetic power to mark her baby while he was still in the womb. All the evidence Stevenson has collected does not prove reincarnation. It only suggests it is possible. Meanwhile, Stevenson continues his research, hoping that one day he will find the "perfect case."

# 8

# A Visit to a Medium

VIRTUALLY EVERY MAJOR METROPOLITAN AREA in the country has its
ample share of professional psychics. They advertise their accom-
plishments in the Yellow Pages or in handbills passed out on the
streets. Some call themselves "Readers," others, "Psychic Mediums." However, most of them work with fortune-telling equipment: cards, crystal ball, or the lines of the palm. To find a psychic
in direct communication with spirits, one must either turn to a
local spiritualist church (also listed in the Yellow Pages) or go
underground and try to contact a spirit medium whose reputation
has spread by word of mouth.

In Washington, D.C., without making an extensive search, I
heard of two different active "spirit circles." But when I asked
(through friends of friends) if I might observe a session, word came
back that I would be a "disruptive influence." I did not pursue the
matter, but instead set up an appointment for a reading with a
woman minister of a "Spiritual Science" church. (The church had
recently been mentioned in the papers as playing host to a
remarkable-sounding healer who claimed to be possessed by the
spirit of a "Princess Tara.")

When I called for the appointment, a secretary asked for my
name and telephone number. I gave them and asked if there
would also be an opportunity to talk to the Reverend about her
work. I explained that I was engaged in a research project. The

secretary said she thought there would be time as I had the last appointment of the day. She also informed me that the "donation" was twenty-five dollars. (This seems to be the going rate in Washington for a private sitting with a spirit medium. Card and palm readers are somewhat cheaper.)

The following day I received a phone call at home reminding me of my appointment. I wondered whether they had taken my name and number to bone up on me before the sitting or whether they received enough crank calls to make checking necessary.

Not knowing what to expect, the next afternoon I drove across town to the residential area where the church was located. It turned out to be a large brownstone house indistinguishable from its neighbors. There was not even a discreet sign above the doorbell to indicate I had arrived at the right place.

A tall middle-aged woman in a flowered caftan answered the door. Her short brown hair was firmly set, but she wore no makeup. She had the pale, abstracted look of a schoolteacher at the end of the day. I mumbled something about an appointment, and she ushered me through the dim hallway, up a wide staircase dripping with plants into a bare-looking room flooded with daylight from three windows. Two wooden chairs stood alone facing each other in the center of the floor. The larger chair had a white shawl draped over its back and, within easy reach, a cassette tape recorder sat on a folding chair.

By this time, I had assumed my hostess was the Reverend herself, for although there had been no introductions, she was unmistakably in charge. Promising to return shortly, she excused herself to get a drink of water. As I peered at the handsomely framed old engravings and maps hung over the bookcases that lined two walls, I wondered if she had left to check out her appointment book. I thought of my car, a beaten-up VW, parked a block away. From the muddy clutter of toys and papers in the back seat, one could reasonably deduce that I was an untidy person who had at least one child and had recently eaten at McDonald's. Would this crop up in my reading?

The Reverend glided back into the room and found me sitting in the smaller chair. I made the motion of getting up, and she sang out, "No, don't move, you're in exactly the right place. You must be psychic!" She sat down across from me and explained she was going to tape the session for me so I could listen to it later. She told me she had no idea what would be said in the reading, but assured me it would be controlled by the "forces of light."

Was she going to go into a trance? I asked. The suggestion seemed to disturb her. No, she answered. The trance state would leave her open to being taken over by stray spirits. She had no intention of abandoning control of herself because she was responsible for anything that happened. She went on to say she was "clairsentient"—a term I had not come across before, but which she defined as the ability to receive clairvoyant "impressions."

After snapping a brand-new tape into the recorder, she switched on the machine, wrapped herself in the shawl, and closed her eyes. She sat with a straight back, her hands folded in her lap.

"And Father God we thank Thee," she prayed in a rhythmic singsong.

"We thank Thee for the guards, guides, teachers and interpreters, and all those who come in thy name to show us the way, the truth, and the light." Her voice drifted off. Then, her eyes still closed, she launched into a short homily: "As you turn the handle of life, you look into the scene and see the pictures flip. The faster you turn, the better the scene, the slower, the more painful. Then keep your hand on the handle and keep turning, quickly, harmoniously, that you are able to understand better the whole picture. . . . And with time, giving yourself three more months, you will see yet better the total picture. . . ."

The image changed. "What you put in the basket, is ultimately what you take out of the basket. You put in your ideas, you let them incubate, then pull out full-fledged"—her voice wandered off and returned with "projects." "You came this way," she rambled on, "to bring the light of understanding to others. Then to teach is important. . . . Do not stay too long in one place, for there are many areas which need your touch. . . ."

Her words were promising, in fact flattering enough to make me suspicious. She stopped, opened her eyes and looked at me. "This is most interesting," she said conversationally. "Because the scene that I look at, it's as though I want to put you out to teach. . . . I want to put you in a school, and I find that I've got you in the right place. Have you ever been to Germany?"

"Yes," I told her, "in 1962."

"Isn't that interesting? I wanted to ask you that question even from the beginning. I can see you—'62, that's ten, eleven years ago. Well, are you going back to Europe?"

"Possibly," I told her.

"You're going to do a lot of traveling," she insisted. She wanted to send me out "over the water," perhaps to teach, as I was born to teach. Had I ever taught?

I told her I had once taught for two years, but was now working on a book.

"Well, it won't be the last book, because they line up on the shelf." She went back to Germany. "I want to pick you up in a very quaint little scene," she told me. "Now let me give this to you. This is not typically German, it's more Swiss, because I can see you as a milkmaid, and your cheeks are very much fatter with two red dots on each one like a doll." The doll had a Dutch hat, she added.

This suggested to her that I was going to travel through Holland, Belgium, Switzerland, and Germany in the near future. "Or in some way you're going to be connected with them. . . . I can't always pin the spirits down. They give me these things and I know that they're going to come up. Do you ever eat cereal?"

"Cereal?"

"Cereal."

"Yes," I answered.

"What kind of cereal do you eat?"

I told her that I liked a Swiss brand health cereal.

"Thank you," she smiled. I was mystified. "That's exactly what I wanted to know," she continued. "Because I was asking how Switzerland comes in here, and then when they said to me, 'Well, you may not actually go there, but you will know it in another way,' the first thing that popped into my head was what kind of cereal do you eat. You are eating Swiss cereal, you see. I simply asked for a test. And for me to test a spirit is to give you something that you know so that you can have faith in something that you don't know. And you know about the Swiss cereal; therefore, you can have faith in the rest of the message. Because for some people only Sugar Pops would be their line of eating."

I nodded, but felt the "evidence" was slightly ridiculous. She had not told me I ate Swiss cereal; I had told her.

"Do you have a question?" she asked.

"Are you seeing pictures now?" I wondered.

"Pictures? They're *impressions*," she corrected.

She sailed on to the "full-fledged project" which would pop out of my basket. "I will call your book writing a project," she said. She felt it would be part of a four-book series. The books had

134

"happy" green and red and blue and yellow covers. Within ten years, she predicted, they would be translated into German and French.

She was most encouraging. "You can do it," she promised. "It is simply a matter of being extremely patient (which you are not) and being able to dig, to delve. . . ."

Was I or was I not patient? I didn't know. More advice followed, all of it sensible. She saw me being handed a mechanical pencil with many boxes of lead and a giant eraser. Then she jumped to something else.

"I'm picking up another time, another place," she stated. "I would like to explore this with your permission." I nodded, relieved to get on with it.

"I want to go to the year 1200. No," she mused, "that's too early." She decided to plunge in anyway. "First of all, I feel that you have had a male incarnation in the country of Spain." I had been well dressed in courtly ruffles, had ridden a horse in a "suit of beautiful, shining silver armor" somewhere in Florida. "I don't know when de Soto came for the fountain of health or whatever that was, but this is what I pick up."

She also found a "great feeling of sadness." I had been a tragic figure, haunted by quixotic dreams. Gradually my New World venture disillusioned me. I never returned to Spain, but put aside the trappings of knighthood, donned homespun, and began to till the soil.

The Reverend proceeded to draw parallels between my former life and my present existence. "You carry within you," she declared, "a great sadness." She told me that I sorrowed not only for the race of mankind, but for my own life, which was permeated with "a feeling of lack."

This was surprising news, but her narrative was compelling,

and I found myself half accepting it. When she told me I would again, in this life, suffer a great disappointment and walk away from all I had known to begin a new life, I felt quite anxious.

She assured me, however, that in this life, I would go further than I had as a Spanish nobleman. I would "climb out of the sadness and find peace."

She seemed to be nearing the end of the message. She began to weave all the loose threads, the travel she had mentioned earlier, the books, the number 12, into the picture. Suddenly it all seemed a little too pat.

"I wanted to bring you the other incarnation," she added, "because it was so strong that I was sitting here looking at you and all I could see was the helmet, and the silver, and your horse. . . . Have you ever been to Spain?"

"Yes," I told her.

"I would feel that Spain would be a place that would affect you."

I tried to convey that although I had enjoyed the trip, the country had no special significance for me. I told her I would have found it easier to believe that I had lived before in England.

She was unfazed. "There's no way we can prove anything," she said with an indulgent smile. "No way we can say it is incarnation or it is another form of giving you the Now." The Spanish knight, she admitted, might simply be "thoughts and desires" from my own subconscious. "I can only give you what I receive from your own vibrations. That's the way it works. As far as I understand it," she amended. "Usually when I come to an understanding, the rug is pulled out from under my feet and I have to go find another one," she said cheerfully.

"And now I want to move on. Someone is giving me the 'Charge of the Light Brigade.' " She described clouds of dust kicked up by galloping horses. I was to ride through the Valley of Death. "Now to me," she elaborated, "the Valley of Death is what we call life." She saw me riding through life, leaving a lot of people behind, suffering a radical change, but finding Meaning at the end of the road. "And that's what you're looking for. I leave you with that." She closed her eyes. "And Father God we thank Thee," she intoned.

After the "Amen," she flicked off the tape recorder and presented me with the cassette. I thanked her and passed over my twenty-five dollars. The rapport I had felt during the seance faded, but I ventured to ask how her church differed from other spiritualist churches in the area. She informed me that her church taught spiritual *science*. Unscientific spiritualists, she explained, worked with sources on the "astral plane"—with departed relatives and friends. Scientific spiritualists, however, were in touch with higher entities, spirit teachers and guides, who had left the astral life far behind.

I asked her how she had become a medium. She answered vaguely about having studied for years. Then, brightening up, she suggested that I should begin studies. I was rather taken aback. "I can't commit myself," I told her. "Ah, yes," she mused as she glided out of the room, "all that traveling."

I passed her on the stairs, talking to her plants as she watered them. I didn't interrupt, but went on out, picking up a pamphlet at the door. It was entitled "The Wonderful World of the Spirit," and contained a list of church activities. In addition to lectures and "Development Circles," there was a ministerial study program. The eight semesters of courses required for ordination cost $960.

On the way home, I went over my session. It was obvious no one had bothered to research me before the reading. Other than the bit about the cereal, I had received no objective information about my life, no names, dates, or places. The teaching she mentioned might have been an educated guess. I had, after all, told the secretary I was working on a "research project." Even if I had never actually taught, her claim that I was "born to teach" was subjective enough to be safe. I had to admit that the part about "walking away" to embark on a solitary quest for Meaning had shaken me. (It jibed with a romantic fantasy I had entertained for years.) But none of the rest of the message had hit home. On the whole, I had the feeling that the reading had been universal enough to be applicable to almost anyone. It contained all the elements of the fortune-teller's stock spiel: travel across water, success in work, change for the better. There was even a dashing dark stranger—only in this case, he turned out to be me.

Later, I realized how clever the Reverend had been in recording the session for home use. The more I listened to the tape, the easier it became to make her words relevant. At the time of the reading, for example, her "impression" of me as a milkmaid doll seemed nothing more than odd. However, going over the tape, it suddenly occurred to me that as I was three months pregnant with my second child, I might well end up as a "milkmaid" in the not too distant future. Had the "spirits" been punning? Or was the coincidence my own invention?

If the tape had become easier to identify with, it had also become more confusing. While some of her "impressions" could be explained as elaborations on things I had told her, others seemed to have popped up out of the blue. I found it impossible to sort out what she might conceivably have picked up telepathically and what she might have been able to read in my appearance. The Reverend was clearly a highly skilled performer, but I was in no way equipped to judge the nature of the talents.

Some time later I came across some advice set down by the

famous psychical researcher Harry Price. "Believe nothing you see or hear at a seance," he urged prospective sitters. "Inexplicable things *do* happen," he wrote in *Confessions of a Ghost Hunter*, "but it is only after long experience, an extensive training in the technique of testing a medium, and a thorough knowledge in the art of mystification, that one can discriminate between truth and falsehood, illusion and reality."

I had toyed with the idea of visiting a more old-fashioned kind of medium, one who might put me in touch with a familiar spirit, but now felt inclined to save my money. However, for those more curious or adventurous than I, here is Harry Price's list of do's and don't's for a private sitting with a mental medium. (Incidentally, he prefaces his recommendations with the advice that "those who are not well balanced emotionally" should shun mediums "like the plague.")

1. Don't give your name. Call yourself X.
2. Don't make the appointment yourself. Have a friend, unknown to the medium, call for you from a public telephone.
3. Don't drive your own car to the medium's residence. Take a taxi instead.
4. Don't wear a uniform or carry a book. This can give the medium clues. Wear no identifying jewelry (wedding ring, school ring, fraternity pin, or I.D. bracelet). Remove rings several days ahead to let the marks disappear.
5. If you visit in winter and wear an overcoat, empty the pockets and take out labels, or name tags.
6. Don't bring a friend. Go alone. Your friend may unconsciously divulge considerable information about you.
7. Be silent. Let the medium do all the talking. Do not ask questions or answer them. Say you'd rather not answer. If

you want to test a spirit, ask questions like "When did you die?" "How old were you at the time?" "Where were you born?" "Did you have brothers and sisters?"

8. Be courteous. Visit in a spirit of goodwill. Don't try to mislead or trick the medium—it will not get you very far.

9. Do not gossip with the medium after the seance, but leave the house immediately.

To these suggestions, I will add two more. First, settle the price of the sitting beforehand. You don't want to be hit for fifty dollars as you're going out the door. Secondly, don't expect to find any clear-cut evidence either of psychic talent or of the existence of a spirit world. On the other hand, do be prepared to hear things you can't explain.

# 9

# Future Dimensions

EXPLAINING THE PRESENTLY UNEXPLAINABLE is the business of parapsychology, a science devoted to the study of telepathy, clairvoyance, and psychokinesis. Early investigators were primarily concerned with the problem of survival after death. Naturally enough, most of their work was done with spirit mediums. It wasn't until the 1930s, when Duke University in North Carolina launched its pioneer investigations of ESP, that the field broadened its scope. Researchers began assuming that psychic abilities were present in everyone, not just specially gifted mediums. They moved away from the seance table into laboratories where they conducted card-guessing experiments using ordinary people as subjects. The results of these tests were analyzed statistically to find out whether the subjects were guessing above or below the laws of chance.

By the early 1940s, researchers had accumulated a massive body of scientific evidence which indicated that ESP did exist. It seemed to be a normal human ability which worked on the unconscious level. Scientists in other fields, however, were unconvinced. The evidence was strong, points out parapsychologist Robert H. Thouless, but not strong enough to outweigh the initial improbability of organisms reacting to information not coming through the senses.

Despite hostile criticism from traditional scientists, since the

1940s, most investigators in the area have accepted ESP as a proven reality. Research is now generally directed toward finding out how and why it works. The field has again branched out. Advances in our technology have inspired new methods as well as new areas of interest. The discovery of LSD in the early sixties, for instance, prompted some researchers to explore the effect of mind-expanding drugs on ESP. Although investigations were dropped after LSD was declared illegal, experimenters turned up no clear-cut evidence that psychedelic drugs boosted ESP performance.

Other researchers, stimulated by the widespread industrial use of electronic computers, have developed computerized ESP tests. In France, parapsychologists have obtained successful test results using an IBM Port-a-Punch computer. In this country, Dr. Helmut Schmidt, a research physicist formerly employed by Boeing Aircraft in Seattle, has invented his own machine for testing precognition—the ability to predict the future. The machine not only generates series of random numbers for the subject to guess, but has an automatic voice which immediately tells the subject the correct answers. (In traditional person-to-person testing, the subject often has to wait weeks before he learns his score.) Since Dr. Schmidt's device is supposed to have built-in safeguards against human error, it may well prove to be a breakthrough for experimenters.

Space explorations have also added a new dimension to parapsychology. Apollo 14 astronaut Edgar Mitchell, mentioned earlier in connection with Arthur Ford, was the first man to perform an ESP experiment in outer space. Without NASA's approval, Mitchell used his rest periods during the moon flight to send ESP test symbols back to earthbound sensitives. Although the experiment had no outstanding results, it did fire the imagination of professional parapsychologists.

At the 1972 annual convention of the Parapsychological Association at Duke University, several prominent speakers stressed the importance of joining hands with NASA teams. Karlis Osis of the American Society for Psychical Research called ESP experiments in space "a must." He believes that such experiments might help solve questions about the nature of ESP. Can it, for example, span the vast distances of outer space? Is it influenced by the earth's gravity field? Would it work when the experimental spaceship was in orbit behind the moon and inaccessible to radio communication?

Another speaker, Joseph H. Rush of Colorado, suggested that in looking for answers to these questions, parapsychologists might well make some totally unexpected discoveries. Christopher Columbus, he argued, "blundered onto America when he was only looking for a better trade route to India."

As for space program scientists, Rush predicted that as they continue their explorations, they will begin to take ESP more seriously. Early in 1972, he pointed out, an unmanned spacecraft left earth for a flight beyond the solar system. It is expected to reach Jupiter, some 500 million miles away, by 1974. As it passes Jupiter, its radio signals will take about forty minutes to reach earth. By the time it reaches Pluto, communication will take about six hours. Rush suggested that as radio communication becomes "steadily more cumbersome and frustrating," scientists will turn to ESP for a possible method of instantaneous communication.

If today's parapsychologists are looking to the future, they have also turned to the past. Several areas of study which were ignored for decades are now being reexamined. By the 1930s, for example, investigations into the connection between psychic ability and hypnosis came to a standstill for lack of positive evidence. Recently, however, interest in hypnosis has revived, and a number of researchers have begun using hypnosis in ESP experiments. They report that hypnotic suggestion does seem to increase ESP performance. Although they have not yet been able to discover how or why, their initial findings suggest that the early hypnotic experimenters described in Chapter 1 were not off base when they claimed that hypnosis produced telepathy and clairvoyance.

Parapsychologists have also begun probing into the age-old mysteries of dreaming. For centuries, mediums and mystics have respected dreams as a channel for psychic revelations. Edgar Cayce, for instance, was particularly interested in dreams. In fact, he taught that dreams were a far better way to get messages from the dead than seances. Although parapsychologists have long recognized that the majority of ordinary people's psychic experiences occur in dreams, until lately they had no method of studying the dream state.

Now, since medical science has shown it is possible to monitor dreams on an EEG (brain wave) machine, the situation has changed. Investigators are able not only to see when a sleeper's dream begins and ends, but to find out what it was about. They have found that if a sleeper is awakened immediately after the dream is over, he is almost always able to remember what he dreamt.

In his book, *ESP Research Today*, the internationally respected parapsychologist J. Gaither Pratt describes some telepathic dream experiments being conducted at the Psychiatry Department of Maimonides Hospital in Brooklyn, New York. After a subject is selected, he arrives at the hospital on the appointed night and goes to bed in an assigned room. In the room next door is an EEG machine. The experimenter hooks him up to it by attaching electrodes to his face and skull, then leaves him alone to go to sleep in a normal way. Meanwhile the experimenter watches the machine in the adjoining room.

As soon as the experimenter sees that his subject has begun to dream, he pushes a button which sets off an electric buzzer in a room in another wing of the hospital. In that room is a person who has been chosen to try to influence the sleeper's dream telepathically. When he hears the buzzer, he begins to concentrate upon a vivid painting he has selected at random. Mentally he asks the sleeper to dream about it.

When the sleeper stops dreaming, the experimenter gives the sender another buzz telling him to relax. The experimenter then wakes up the subject by calling him on a two-way intercom. The subject relates his dream, which is recorded on tape, then goes back to sleep. This procedure continues throughout the night whenever the subject dreams.

After eight nights of this, the experimenter has a total of eight different pictures and eight sets of dreams. These are scrambled and given to an outside panel of judges who try to match the subject's dreams with the pictures. When the results have been analyzed statistically, it has been found that the dreams resemble the pictures often enough to suggest that telepathy has been at work.

In some instances the similarity between the dreams and the pictures has been amazingly close. Pratt reports that at a parapsychological convention, the Maimonides researchers projected a slide showing a painting of a boxing scene which had been used in the experiments. At the same time, they read the subject's account of his dream. According to Pratt, the subject's dream was "so vivid and so accurate in detail" that it was difficult to see how anyone could have given a better description of the picture even while looking at it.

Although research into dreams and telepathy is still in its initial stages, Pratt feels confident enough to conclude: "On the basis of hard data and solid scientific evidence, we can now accept it as demonstrated fact that one person's thoughts can in some way, directly and at a distance, influence another person's dream." Thus, if you suddenly dream about a close friend you haven't seen in a long time, it may be more than a memory. It's just possible that your friend may have been sending you a message.

If, as Pratt suggests, "Science must now take seriously some of the old and persistent beliefs about dreams," it has already begun to respect the no less primitive claim that man can communicate with plants and animals. As discussed in Chapter 5, in the late 1930s, Kirlian photography in Russia confirmed the mediumistic assertion that all living things have an aura. Recent experiments, however, indicate that animals and plants have even more in common with man. Not only are they surrounded by the same energy field, but they appear to have ESP as well.

In the 1950s, at Duke University, investigators began examining certain patterns of animal behavior. Numerous reports, for example, that pet animals had trailed their masters to new, far-away locations indicated that animals had some kind of ESP power. But researchers were not able to reach any final conclusions. Now, new evidence to support their theory has been found in laboratory experiments with rats and mice.

In France, for example, zoologists tested the ability of mice to predict the future by using a specially designed automatic cage. The cage was divided in half by a low partition. Each half of its floor was wired to produce a mild electric shock. The mouse was put inside the cage, and current was applied randomly to one side or the other. Experiments found that the mice appeared to be able to foresee which side the shock would hit and to avoid it by jumping over the partition.

Parapsychologists in this country have had successful results from similar experiments. They also are engaged in testing ESP in plants. But the first person to discover that plants can "read" people's minds was not a parapsychologist, but a CIA lie detector expert named Cleve Backster. One day in 1966, Backster was watering the plants in his New York office when he decided to try hooking one up to a galvanometer, a machine which electronically records emotional charges given off by human beings. He attached electrodes to its leaves, watered it, and after thirty seconds, saw the machine trace a contour that in a human being would have indicated emotional excitement.

Curious, he decided to try burning one of the plant's leaves. But before he could reach for a match, the machine's recording pen bounced off the chart. The plant reacted to the threat of pain in the same way as a human being would. Further trials yielded even more startling results. When Backster simply pretended he was going to burn the leaf, the plant was unperturbed.

As Backster continued his experiments, he found that plants became fearful when other living things were harmed. When, for example, he killed live shrimp by dumping them in boiling water, the plants in the room made violent patterns on the galvanometer's chart. He also discovered that when plants themselves were faced with overwhelming danger, they "fainted," registering a blank on the machine.

On one occasion, the plants in his office "passed out" when a woman physiologist came to see his experiments. A puzzled Backster asked the woman if she used plants in her work. She admitted she did and explained that at the end of her experiments, she destroyed all her plants. She roasted them in an oven to obtain their dry weight. It wasn't until forty-five minutes after she was safely out of his office that Backster's plants began to revive.

If plants can recognize their enemies, they also seem to know their friends. Other experiments showed that plants appear to have a special bond with their caretakers. Backster found that even separated by three thousand miles, plants had instantaneous reactions to their keeper's thoughts and feelings. "We're in another dimension," says Backster, "a scientific twilight in which something can go from point to point without going in between and without consuming time to get there."

Backster's discoveries have inspired other researchers to make their own tests. *Harper's Magazine* reported in November, 1972, that Paul Sauvin, an electronics technician and inventor, has built a device which enabled a philodendron in his laboratory to trigger a radio signal. When, from a distance two miles away from his lab, Sauvin sent the plant a strong emotion, the plant responded by activating the radio signal which, in turn, started the engine of a car parked outside the laboratory. Sauvin is looking forward to the day when people can command their plants to open their garage door for them on sleety days.

*Harper's* also described the work of Marcel Vogel, an IBM research chemist, who found that plants have definite tastes in music. They flourished, for example, while listening to Bach, but withered and eventually died under constant blasts of acid rock. Vogel also found that plants reacted to human conversations. Talk about engineering seemed to bore them, but when the topic of sex came up, the plants suddenly perked up. This led Vogel to speculate that ancient fertility rites may actually have stimulated the growth of crops.

Vogel's experiments, however, have taught him that the best food for plants is love. This is something that green-thumbed gardeners know intuitively, but it has been recently demonstrated in a miraculous-sounding experiment being carried out on the barren, windblown east coast of Scotland. There, on a half acre of

*These strip chart recordings of variations of a DC voltage across groups of plant cells were taken by Paul Sauvin. The recording at left was produced by a plant located thirty feet from a human being in a normal emotional state; the plant recorded at right was located thirty feet from a human being in a highly emotional, anxious state.*

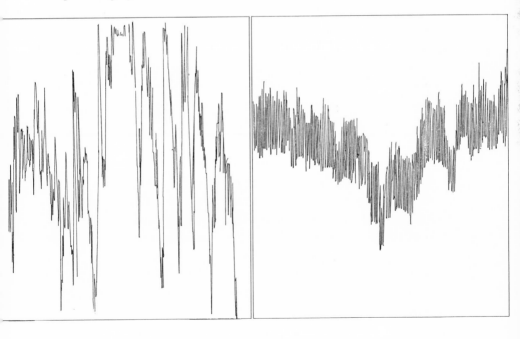

soil composed mostly of sand and gravel, two plant lovers named Peter and Elixir Caddy have raised abundant crops of fruits and vegetables in mid-winter.

Although agricultural experts who visited the Caddys were unable to explain why their plants bloomed so vigorously in such worthless soil, the Caddys themselves say love is the secret. They claim that each plant species has its own guardian spirit. When gardeners raise their plants with love and joy, the spirit is pleased and does its best to produce beautiful fruits and flowers. The Caddys are confident that by entering into communication with plant spirits, man can restore our ecologically devastated planet to a Garden of Eden.

Parapsychologists are also optimistic about the future. But unlike spiritualists, who seem to know the deeper secrets of the cosmos, they are still searching for explanations. As Pratt points out in his book on ESP research, "Parapsychology is not for miracle-seekers nor for those who demand instant answers." It is a field, he declares, for open-minded scientists. Pratt cautions that only science can help parapsychology sift out fact from fantasy. Only further research can replace superstition with sound knowledge. Such an achievement, he believes, can not help but improve the future.

# Suggestions for Further Reading

The following list of general works is provided for readers who wish to pursue particular subjects dealt with or mentioned in passing in this book. All of these books are likely to be found in large libraries, and many contain excellent bibliographies of less accessible primary sources.

Bro, Harmon Hartzell. *Edgar Cayce on Dreams.* New York: Hawthorne Books, 1968. (Paperback edition: Paperback Library.)

One of the many "Edgar Cayce on" books published under the auspices of the ARE. Other titles in the series range from *Edgar Cayce on Atlantis* to *Edgar Cayce on the Dead Sea Scrolls.* (Paperback editions: Paperback Library.)

Burton, Jean. *Heyday of a Wizard.* New York: A. A. Knopf, 1944.

Elegant, entertaining biography of Daniel Home. Useful bibliography.

Ford, Arthur. *Nothing So Strange.* New York: Harper & Brothers, 1958.

Ford is often candid in this highly readable autobiography, but by no means "tells all." His account in Chapter 15 of an out-of-the-body trip to an after-death "Judgement Hall" is particularly noteworthy.

Fornell, Earl Wesley. *The Unhappy Medium.* Austin: University of Texas Press, 1964.

A carefully documented account of Maggie Fox's career and "Rappomania" with many colorful tidbits and an excellent bibliography.

Garrett, Eileen J. *Many Voices: The Autobiography of a Medium.* New York: Putnam, 1968.

The final and most well-rounded of several autobiographical works by one of the most tested mediums of the century.

Monroe, Robert A. *Journeys Out of the Body.* New York: Doubleday, 1971. (Paperback edition: Doubleday.)

A searching, first-hand account of experiments in astral projection. Complete with do-it-yourself tips.

Ostrander, Sheila & Schroeder, Lynn. *Psychic Discoveries Behind the Iron Curtain.* Englewood Cliffs: Prentice-Hall, 1970. (Paperback edition: Bantam Books.)

Enthusiastic reporting on the Russian parapsychological scene. Many Western researchers regard the book skeptically.

Pike, James A. *The Other Side.* Garden City: Doubleday, 1968.

Bishop Pike's own account of his experiences with psychic phenomena.

Pratt, J. Gaither. *Parapsychology: An Insider's View of ESP.* Garden City: Doubleday, 1964.

One of the world's foremost parapsychologists relates his own experiences in ESP research. Includes a chapter on animals and ESP.

————. *ESP Research Today: A Study of Developments in Parapsychology Since 1960.* Metuchen: Scarecrow Press, 1973.

Pratt brings the reader up to date on the latest research in the field. Includes chapters on Russian parapsychology and a list of books for supplemental reading.

Price, Harry. *Fifty Years of Psychical Research*. London: Longmans, Green & Co., 1939.

The famous pioneering psychic investigator chronicles the still unsolved mysteries of his work with some remarkable twentieth-century mediums.

Roberts, Jane. *The Seth Material*. Englewood Cliffs: Prentice-Hall, 1970. (Paperback edition: Prentice-Hall.)

Roberts' story of her first encounters with the "spirit-guide" Seth.

Spraggett, Allan. *Arthur Ford, the Man Who Talked with the Dead*. New York: New American Library, 1973.

A critical appraisal of the medium's career by a seasoned observer of the psychic scene. Includes detailed accounts of both the Houdini affair and the Bishop Pike seance. Excellent bibliography.

Stearn, Jess. *Search for the Girl with the Blue Eyes*. Garden City: Doubleday, 1968. (Paperback edition: Bantam Books.)

Stearn has authored many popular books on the occult, including *Edgar Cayce, the Sleeping Prophet* (Doubleday, 1967. Paperback edition: Bantam Books). Here he gives a first-hand account of his experiences with Canadian teenager Joanne MacIver who discovered through hypnosis that she had lived once before in the past.

Sugre, Thomas. *There Is a River*. New York: H. Holt & Co., 1945.

The official story of Edgar Cayce's life written by one of his friends. Pious, but painlessly informative, with an appendix of six case histories illustrating Cayce's method of psychic diagnosis.

# Index

# About the Author

CHRISTINE ANDREAE, teacher and free-lance journalist, has written many articles for the *Washingtonian* and the *Washington Star*. SEANCES & SPIRITUALISTS is her first book. She and her husband, an architect, live with their two young children in Washington, D.C., and Bentonville, Virginia.